Intermittent Fa

for Women Over 50

A Complete Guide to Help you Learn about the Science behind Intermittent Fasting, its Advantages and Different Protocols for Women over 50

AILEEN WILLIAMSON

Table of Contents

Introduction

Diet pills were common in the 1990s. You were losing out on life's quintessential fitness boosts if you didn't get a juicer in the early 2000s. Green tea pads that minimize tummy size have been sent to us; even if you're not eating like a Neanderthal, you're still at a disadvantage. If something is marketed as new and game-changing in weight reduction, it's primarily marketing to promote whatever is now famous. If there was ever a fad to get behind, it's intermittent fasting.

Intermittent fasting is a form of calorie restriction that requires a series of on-and-off intervals of feeding. We know it seems dull and easy, but believe us, we soon learned that it is a self-discipline practice that can be exhausting at first when we started it.

We've spent the bulk of 2019 practicing intermittent fasting, and the benefits we've had involve weight loss, mental stability, a good night's sleep, and a lot more control. We began struggling with intermittent fasting for the sake of health, rather than weight loss. But the first thing we found was that belly fat had significantly decreased. Since you can't spot-reduce fat on your body, the loss of belly fat would have been due to hormones. As we all recognize, weight gain in the midsection is a part of existence after menopause.

Intermittent fasting is a tool that people we admire and follow in our lifespan, use to remain younger. Prof David Sinclair of Harvard University, a longevity scientist and expert, placed their mind at ease when he said that no one knows the exact solution or the optimal way of fasting, even though they pretend to. Experiments on mice have shown that consuming 30% less food, increases lifespan by 30%.

Another part of intermittent fasting that we find intriguing and ground-breaking is its anti-aging efficacy and the benefits it brings to longevity. This is primarily accomplished by autophagy, which is the body's normal means of eliminating weakened cells and repairing them with fresh, stable ones. It's like recycling. This is highly promising in terms of long-term sustainability. It is a safe, natural way to replace old cells and switch back the clock with the development of new ones. Autophagy is a natural process that our ancestors instilled in us to provide nutrition to the body (self-eating). Of course, this won't continue forever because you'll be feeding all day, the body won't be able to sustain it. When our cells get nervous, intermittent fasting increases autophagy. Autophagy is enabled to defend and replenish the body.

It's not easy to adjust to intermittent fasting, mainly if you're doing it all at once. One factor we could refrain from during our feeding times is bingeing on vast quantities of unhealthy foods. It's possible not to get any results if we do this. First and foremost, we suggest that you change your eating patterns. Before undertaking extended fasting, settling into a habit of eating as healthily as practicable would be incredibly helpful. We recommend you start doing this two weeks before deciding to start your intermittent fasting routine, which will make the transition far smoother.

While you're fasting, you shouldn't take any vitamins because your body needs to do all the work independently. When we break our fast, the first thing we eat is protein. It has little to do with fat or carbohydrates. This results in a good impact on our body.

Discover an excellent fitness idea for women over 50 that they can quickly adapt to. When a woman tries to lose weight, she typically begins limiting her calorie consumption in the morning; at lunch, and she attempts to compromise for a salad or a small snack, or even miss the meal to conserve calories; then in the evening, appetite builds up, bursting at dinner.

The quickest way to add weight is to feed less throughout the day and a lot at night. Hunger, like sleep, builds up during the day, bursting in the late hours, when our metabolism is at its least effective.

Instead, the most recent research findings on weight loss indicate that removing, or at the very least decreasing the calories in the evening meal, even though just for a limited time, has been successful in weight loss and overall health improvement.

Chapter 1: What Is Intermittent Fasting?

Intermittent fasting is a type of eating habit, in which you only eat for a certain amount of time.

Fasting may be achieved in several forms. Some people feed all day and fast for most of the night. For example, you might eat for 8 hours a day, say from 12 p.m. to 8 p.m., and fast for the remaining 16. Others prefer to consume a standard diet-specific day of the week and fast, or eat, a minimum number of calories on others.

Why do you deny yourself? Intermittent fasting is justified for a variety of purposes.

Evidence shows that while cells are stressed by not feeding, they might prevent disease. Fasting can also decrease inflammation in the body and sugar levels, cholesterol levels, and blood pressure. And, of course, there's a lot of study on weight reduction from intermittent fasting.

When you don't feed, the body taps into its fat reserves for nutrition. Fasting over a fixed amount of time will help you reduce weight by lowering the average calorie intake.

Adults in a study observed alternate day fasting, in which they usually fed on alternate days, but only consumed 20% of their daily calories on the other days. In only eight weeks, the bulk of the subjects had lost 8% of their body weight.

Intermittent fasting (IF) is one of the most common health and wellness phenomena in the world right now. People are using it to lose weight, boost their wellbeing, and ease their lives. Many tests have demonstrated that it may positively influence the body and brain, and that it can also help you live longer.

Intermittent fasting is eating that interchanges between fasting and eating times. It doesn't tell you what foods to eat, but rather when you can eat them. In this way, it's more aptly defined as an eating routine instead of a diet in the traditional sense.

Humans have practiced fasting since the beginning of time. Supermarkets, refrigerators, and year-round food were not open to ancient hunter-gatherers. They couldn't find anything to consume. Therefore, humans have naturally adapted to be able to survive for long periods without food.

Fasting is, in effect, more normal than consuming 3–4 (or more) meals a day, daily. Fasting is also practiced in Islam, Christianity, Judaism, and Buddhism for theological or moral purposes. Many diets emphasize what to eat, but intermittent fasting emphasizes when to eat.

Intermittent fasting is where you feed during a limited time of the day. Fasting for a certain number of hours per day or consuming just one meal a couple of times a week, will aid in weight loss. Scientific research also suggests that there are certain health advantages.

Mark Mattson, Ph.D., a neuroscientist at Johns Hopkins University, has practiced intermittent fasting for 25 years. He claims that our bodies have adapted to go out without nutrients for many hours, days, or even weeks. Before humans learned to plant, they were hunter-gatherers who adapted to live—and flourish—without feeding over lengthy periods. They needed to: Hunting game and gathering nuts and berries required a lot of time and effort.

It was simpler to keep a healthier weight also 50 years earlier. "There were no phones, only TV programs shut off at 11 p.m.; people avoided consuming before they went to bed," says Christie Williams, M.S., R.D.N., a dietitian at Johns Hopkins. "The portions were considerably lower. More residents exercised and played outdoors, getting more exercise in general."

"Television, the telephone, and other forms of content are now accessible 24 hours a day, seven days a week. We remain up later to watch our favorite movies, play sports, and talk on the internet. We spend the whole day—and much of the night—sitting and snacking." Obesity, type 2 diabetes, heart failure, and other diseases may also be exacerbated from eating so many calories and doing so little. Intermittent fasting has been seen in scientific trials to further change these phenomena.

1.1 The Science Behind Intermittent Fasting

A lot of convincing intermittent fasting (IF) research has been conducted on fat rats. They lose weight, have lower cholesterol, blood pressure, and blood sugar levels, but they're rats. Furthermore, many people find fasting a challenge.

However, an increasing body of evidence shows that quick pacing is crucial, making it a more practical, manageable, and reliable weight loss and diabetes prevention strategy.

The world is becoming increasingly chubby. It's a global trend, but one that's particularly evident in the United States. According to government figures, 42% of people in the United States were obese in 2018, almost three times higher than in 1980 and previous decades. As a result, serious health problems such as diabetes, atherosclerosis, heart attacks, and strokes are rising.

One explanation for all this weight growth is that Americans eat more calories: national data suggests a 200-calorie rise per day between the early 1970s and 2010. One reason is so many people are snacking as they've never snacked before. In 2010, US adults ingested around 20% more calories from sweets than they did in the early 1970s, and many no longer enjoy the usual three meals a day. In a 2015 survey of 156 US adults, it was discovered that the majority fed more than four meals per day, with some eating up to 15 times, on average.

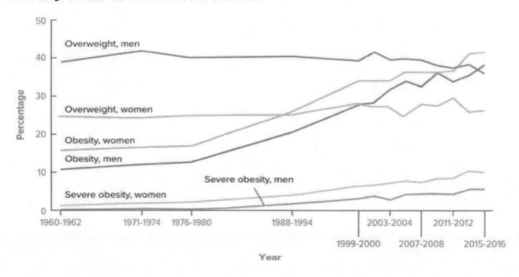

However, a growing majority of experts believe that obesity is caused by more than just constant grazing. Timing is also essential: we eat when we shouldn't and don't allow our bodies enough time between meals.

According to Dominic D'Agostino, a neurobiologist at the University of South Florida, who examines the impact of diet on the brain, we didn't grow to consume such few meals during the day and night. On the other side, humans also adapted to cope with daily fasts: We survived hunting and collecting until the advent of agriculture about 12,000 years ago, and we mostly had to do so with hollow bellies. "We are hard-wired to endure occasional intermittent fasting," D'Agostino notes.

Furthermore, according to Satchin Panda at the Salk Institute (a circadian biologist), in La Jolla, California, who published an analysis on the timing of feeding in the 2019 Annual Examination of Nutrition, people are consuming at times of the day when they may have been asleep traditionally. He argues that for thousands of years, our nighttime fast began far sooner than it does now, in the era of late-night television and other electric-powered diversions that enable us to sit up late and snack through the wee hours.

People typically eat for more than 12 hours each day

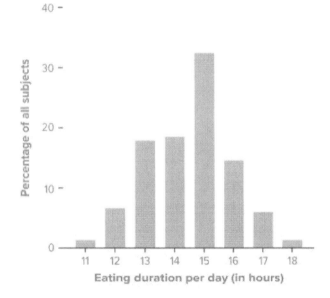

Studies are beginning to say that the scheduling of meals affects body weight and wellbeing.

Such habits, which have drawn thousands of adherents and are frequently referred to as "intermittent fasting," seem to help prevent obesity and may change the body's metabolism in beneficial ways, according to supporters. More speculatively, animal experiments show that the diets can boost athletic stamina and memory, improve diabetes, and possibly even help prevent or slow disease progression like cancer and Alzheimer's disease.

More study into time-restricted eating is needed. There haven't been any human subjects' trials that have lasted more than a couple of months so far. Fasting's effects on the human body must also be understood, according to researchers. The gut microbiota, for example, has been shown to shift in mice who limit their feeding to an eight-to-nine-hour span, allowing them to consume nutrients differently and ingest less sugar and fat.

Intermittent fasting isn't a magic weight-loss remedy. According to some studies, people who follow the 5:2 diet or alternative fasting can instinctively eat extra before and after their fasting days and minimize their exercise on fasting days, eliminating the calorie-cutting benefits.

A time-restricted diet has a range of benefits over most weight loss types: It's easy and straightforward. Diets have the disadvantage of managing them, since many people don't have the patience or money to count calories, prepare their menus, purchase certain ingredients, and log their calories. Anyone who can count hours, and restrict eating and drinking to fixed times, can practice time-restricted eating.

People who wish to lose weight have had to concentrate on modifying their regular menus for a long time. Time-restricted feeding can broaden the range of variables under our influence.

1.2 Benefits of Intermittent Fasting for Women Over age 50

Intermittent fasting is an eating practice under which you alternate between eating and fasting times. It can be achieved in several forms, such as the 16/8 or 5:2 techniques. Numerous tests have demonstrated that it can have significant health and cognitive effects. Here are ten health effects of prolonged fasting that have been scientifically proven.

1. Intermittent Fasting Changes the Function of Cells, Genes, and Hormones

When you don't feed for a period of time, the body goes through a lot of shifts.

To render accumulated body fat more available, the body, for example, initiates essential cellular repairing processes and adjusts hormone levels.

Here are some of the physiological modifications that arise during fasting:

- Insulin levels: Insulin levels in the blood decrease dramatically, facilitating fat burning.

- Human growth hormone: Growth hormone levels in the blood will rise by up to 5-fold. Increased amounts of this hormone aid with weight loss and muscle growth, among other things.

- Cellular repair: The body initiates critical cellular repair procedures, such as removing waste from cells.

- Gene expression: There are favorable variations in various genes and molecules tied to survival and disease prevention.

These shifts in hormones, gene expression, and cell structure, are attributed to many of the advantages of intermittent fasting.

2. Intermittent Fasting Can Help You Lose Weight and Belly Fat

Many people who experiment with intermittent fasting do so to reduce weight.

Besides, extended fasting allows you to consume fewer meals.

You can need fewer calories, unless you compensate for consuming even more during the other meals.

Intermittent fasting often improves hormone function, which aids weight reduction.

Low insulin levels, high growth hormone levels, and higher norepinephrine (noradrenaline) levels help the body break down fat and use it for energy. Therefore, short-term fasting raises your metabolic rate by 3.7-13%, enabling you to eat more calories.

Intermittent fasting, in other words, operates on all sides of the calorie calculation. It raises the metabolic rate (calories expended), thereby decreasing the quantity of food you consume (reduces calories). According to a 2014 study of the clinical literature, intermittent fasting will result in weight loss of 3-8% over 3-24 weeks. This is a large number.

The subjects have lost 4-7% of their waist circumference, suggesting they lost a lot of belly fat, the disease-causing fat in the abdominal cavity. Intermittent fasting also induced less muscle damage than constant calorie restriction, according to a review report.

3. Intermittent Fasting Can Lower Insulin Resistance, Lowering Your Probability of Type 2 Diabetes

In recent decades, type 2 diabetes has become extremely widespread.

High blood sugar in the sense of insulin resistance is the most prominent characteristic. Something that decreases insulin tolerance and defends against type 2 diabetes should help reduce blood sugar levels.

Intermittent fasting has been found to have significant benefits for insulin tolerance and a significant decrease in blood sugar levels. It has been indicated to lower fasting blood sugar by 3.5-6% and fasting insulin by 21-31% in human trials. Intermittent fasting often prevented diabetic rats from kidney injury, one of the most dangerous consequences of diabetes.

This means that intermittent fasting could be very beneficial for individuals at risk of having type 2 diabetes. There might, still, be specific gender disparities. According to one report, during a 22-day intermittent fasting regimen, blood sugar management in women worsened.

4. Intermittent Fasting Can Lower Down Oxidative Stress and Inflammation in The Body

One of the moves against aging and multiple chronic illnesses is oxidative stress. It entails reactive molecules such as free radicals interfering with and destroying other essential molecules (such as protein and DNA).

Intermittent fasting has been shown in some trials to improve the body's tolerance to oxidative stress. Research indicates that intermittent fasting may help combat inflammation, which is a significant cause of several diseases.

5. Intermittent Fasting May be Useful for Heart Health

Heart attack is still the world's leading cause of death. Various health indicators (also known as "danger factors") have been related to an elevated or reduced cardiac failure risk.

Intermittent fasting has also been shown to increase blood pressure, blood triglycerides, total and LDL cholesterol, inflammation receptors, and blood sugar levels, among other risk factors. However, a significant portion of this is focused on animal research. Before any decisions can be developed, further research on the impact on humans' heart health is needed.

6. Intermittent Fasting Stimulates Various Repair Cellular Processes

When we fast, our bodies' cells start a process called autophagy, which is a cellular "waste removal" process. Broken and damaged proteins that accumulate within cells over time are broken down and metabolized by the cells. Increased autophagy can protect against cancer and Alzheimer's disease, among other diseases.

7. Intermittent Fasting May Help Prevent Cancer

Cancer is a horrific disease that is marked by uncontrollable cell development.

Fasting has been found to have a variety of biochemical advantages, including a decreased incidence of cancer. Intermittent fasting can help reduce cancer, according to encouraging results from animal trials. Human studies are required.

Fasting minimized multiple side effects of chemotherapy in human cancer patients, according to some evidence.

8. Intermittent Fasting is Good for Your Brain

What is healthy for the body is frequently also beneficial for the brain.

Intermittent fasting increases several biochemical characteristics that are linked to brain health. Reduced oxidative stress, inflammation, blood sugar levels, and insulin tolerance are all part of this.

Intermittent fasting has been shown in rats' experiments to accelerate the development of innovative nerve cells, which could boost brain activity. It often boosts amounts of a brain hormone named brain-derived neurotrophic factor (BDNF), which has been linked to depression and other mental illnesses.

Intermittent fasting has also been found to protect against brain injury caused by strokes in animals.

9. Intermittent Fasting May Help Out to Prevent Alzheimer's Disease

The most prevalent neurodegenerative disorder in the world is Alzheimer's disease. Since there is no treatment for Alzheimer's disease, preventing it from occurring is crucial.

According to a rat report, intermittent fasting can postpone the onset of Alzheimer's disease or minimize its intensity. A dietary intervention that involved regular short-term fasts substantially enhanced Alzheimer's symptoms in 8 out of 10 patients, according to a collection of case studies.

According to animal research, fasting may also guard against some neurodegenerative disorders, such as Parkinson's and Huntington's disease. However, further human testing is needed.

10. Intermittent Fasting May Expand Your Lifespan, Assisting You In Living Longer

One of the most intriguing aspects of intermittent fasting is the capacity to prolong life expectancy.

Intermittent fasting increases longevity in rats in the same manner as constant calorie restriction would. The results of some of these experiments were theatrical. One found that rats who fasted every day lived 83% longer than rats who didn't fast.

Intermittent fasting has been very common with the anti-aging community because it has yet to be demonstrated in humans. With the effects of intermittent fasting for metabolism and various health indicators, it's easy to see how it might help you live a longer and happier life.

Intermittent fasting does more than burn fat, according to research. "Changes in this metabolic switch influence the body and the brain," Mattson says. Here are some of the effects of intermittent fasting that have been discovered so far in research:

- Memory and thinking skills: Intermittent fasting improves cognitive function in animals and verbal fluency in adults, according to research.

- Cardiovascular wellbeing: Fasting over a brief amount of time increases blood pressure, sleeping heart rates, and other heart-related metrics.

- Physical abilities: Fasting for 16 hours culminated in weight reduction while retaining muscle mass in young males. Mice that were fed on various days had increased running stamina.

- Obesity and diabetes: Intermittent fasting has been found to prevent obesity in livestock. In six small trials, obese adult humans shed weight by fasting intermittently.

- The condition of the tissues: Intermittent fasting in animals, minimized tissue injury during treatment and increased outcomes.

1.3 Drawbacks of Intermittent Fasting for Women Over 50

This study's noteworthy feature was the high rate of dropout (38%) for those allocated to the fasting protocol. This may be a real-life example of the risks of fasting as a weight-loss technique. "It's human instinct for people to want to motivate themselves after putting in a lot of effort, such as exercising or fasting for a long time," Dr. Hu explains, "so there's a risk of indulging in poor eating patterns on non-fasting days." Furthermore, there is a powerful biological drive to overeat during fasting times. When you're hungry, the appetite receptors and hunger core in your brain go into overdrive.

Several commercial firms are also selling packaged meal menus tailored exclusively for intermittent fasting. Though this can make the task smoother for others, these items are usually very costly—around $300 for a week's worth of food.

Fasting has been shown to mitigate cancer risk and delay aging in livestock, which has ignited curiosity in intermittent fasting. According to Dr. Hu, "one theory is that fasting will stimulate cellular pathways that help improve immune function and lower down inflammation linked with chronic disease." Suppose it's true, that losing weight improves a person's metabolic balance and lowers cardiovascular risk.

1.4 Who Should Not Try Intermittent Fasting?

If you're worried about attempting intermittent fasting, speak to a doctor first. For those with diseases, such as diabetes, missing meals and drastically reducing calories may be harmful. People who take blood pressure or cardiac condition drugs could be more vulnerable to electrolyte disturbances because of fasting. We still reside in a poisonous, obesogenic food climate, according to Dr. Hu. To sustain low-calorie days over time, you'll need a good social support network.

So far, intermittent fasting seems to have a good impact. However, if a diet isn't approached correctly, it will still have drawbacks. The following are seven possible drawbacks or "cons" to intermittent fasting:

1. Intermittent Fasting can still lead to weight gain

2. Fasting can make you feel tired and moody

3. Skipping meals can cause headaches, dizziness, and nausea

4. Restrictive eating can lead to disordered eating

5. It can be hard to stick with long-term

6. It may affect your social life

7. There's an increased risk for some negative health consequences

Chapter 2: How does Intermittent Fasting Work?

To comprehend how intermittent fasting contributes to fat loss, we must first comprehend the fed and fasted states' distinction.

When the body digests and absorbs food, it is in a fed condition. The fed condition usually begins when you eat and lasts for three to five hours while the body digests and consumes it. It is challenging for the body to burn fat while you are in the fed state.

During that time, the body enters a condition recognized as post-absorptive. The post-absorptive condition continues before you reach the fasted state, which is 8 to 13 hours after your last meal. Since the insulin levels are inadequate, burning fat is even better when you fast. Because of the constant carbohydrate supply, the body will burn fat that was previously unavailable during the fed state, and your sugar levels are intense.

Our bodies are rarely in this fat-burning condition, and we don't reach the fasted state until 12 hours after our last meal. This is one reason why many people who begin intermittent fasting lose weight without altering their diet, amount of food consumed or frequency of exercise. Fasting causes the body to enter a fat-burning mode that is uncommon during a regular feeding routine.

Many other things happen in your body on a cellular and molecular basis. To make processed body fat more available, the body changes hormone levels, for example. Essential repair mechanisms and gene expression changes are often initiated by your cells.

During a short fast, your body undergoes the following changes:

- Human Growth Hormone (HGH): Growth hormone levels spike, often by as many as 5-fold. This has advantages in terms of weight reduction and muscle gain, among other items.

- Insulin: Insulin response increases, and insulin levels decrease substantially. Insulin levels that are lower allow accumulated body fat more available.

- Cellular repair: As you fast, your cells begin to repair themselves. Autophagy is a process in which cells ingest and destroy old and inactive proteins accumulated within them.

- Gene expression: There are variations in gene regulation that are attributed to survival and disease tolerance.

Intermittent fasting's health advantages are improvements in hormone levels, cell structure, and gene expression. Intermittent fasting may result in an automatic decrease of calorie consumption, resulting in weight loss by altering both calorie equation aspects.

It raises the fat-burning hormone norepinephrine production, reduces insulin, and raises growth hormone levels (noradrenaline). Short-term fasting can raise your metabolic rate by 3.7–14% due to these hormonal changes.

This eating pattern will result in a 2–8% weight loss across 3–24 weeks, according to a 2014 analysis report, which is a significant amount compared to other weight loss studies.

According to the same report, people have lost 3–7% of their waist circumference, suggesting a substantial loss of unhealthy belly fat that builds up around the organs and induces illness.

In another analysis, intermittent fasting induced more minor muscle weakness than the more common form of constant calorie restriction.

Bear in mind, though, that the fundamental explanation for its popularity is that intermittent fasting lets you consume fewer calories overall. You do not suffer the loss of much weight if you indulge and consume more through your feeding hours.

Intermittent fasting may be achieved in several forms, but they revolve around choosing daily food and fasting hours. For example, you might consider eating just for eight hours a day and fasting for the rest of the day. Alternatively, you might opt to consume just one meal a day, two days a week. There are a variety of intermittent fasting routines to choose from.

According to Mattson, after some time without carbohydrates, the body's sugar reserves are depleted, and it begins to burn fat. He refers to this as metabolic flipping.

"Most Americans feed in their waking hours, but prolonged fasting is in comparison to their usual feeding pattern," Mattson notes. "If somebody consumes three meals a day with treats and doesn't work out, they're living on some calories and not burning their fat reserves any time they eat."

Intermittent fasting operates by extending the time from when the body burns off the calories from your last meal and starts burning fat.

- Intermittent fasting can help people lose weight by reducing overall calorie intake, particularly at night.

- More study is required to learn more about the effects of intermittent fasting on our wellbeing and how it may be utilized to lose weight.

The people who practiced the diet the most explicitly lost the most weight, but others who followed a less stringent intermittent fasting protocol also lost weight.

Intermittent fasting has received mixed reviews in the scientific community. Although several findings have shown that intermittent fasting isn't a significant predictor of weight reduction, most evidence shows that the eating pattern can help with obesity, diabetes, cardiovascular disease, cancer, and neurological disorders.

More study is required to understand more about the implications of intermittent fasting on our wellbeing and how it could be used to lose weight.

2.1 Intermittent Fasting Seems to Help in Weight Loss

For 12 weeks, 50 obese people were required to observe intermittent fasting at the Queen Mary University, London.

Participants were expected to adopt a time-restricted diet, fasting for 16 hours, and consuming all their foods within an 8-hour timeframe. To maintain track of the participants' development, the researchers administered a weekly phone survey. After six weeks, the subjects were weighed again, and after 12 weeks, they were weighed again.

Three months later, 60% of the patients were already on the restrictive diet schedules. They lost a total of 7 pounds, accounting for at least 5% of their body weight.

Many that adhered to the fasting diet loosely shed weight as well. However, this is a limited sample. To better understand how intermittent fasting contributes to weight loss, further study with more participants is required.

2.2 Can Intermittent Fasting Lead to Rapid Loss of Weight?

The 16:8 diet that allows people to fast for 15-16 hours and then eat for only 8 hours is perhaps the most popular intermittent fasting plan.

Intermittent fasting has grown in popularity in recent years, but studies into whether it will help people lose weight have been mixed.

Weight reduction is likely that individuals who practice time-restricted feeding intake fewer calories total, according to Dr. Artur Viana.

"It's doubtful that anyone can consume enough calories in the 8 hours they're permitted to eat to make up for the calories they missed during the sixteen hours of fasting," Viana said.

Intermittent fasting often decreases overnight consumption, according to Dr. John Morton.

"One thing we know for sure is that eating late at night increases the chances of adding weight," Morton added.

It's more challenging to eat calories at night because metabolism slows down, according to Morton.

Intermittent fasting has been shown to improve metabolism in several studies.

"Small studies have indicated that time-restricted eating (TRE) may overcome metabolic adaptation during weight loss (a process that contributes to weight gain), favorably affect body composition against reduced fat mass, decrease appetite, and surge satiety," Viana said, but more extensive studies are required to confirm this.

Fasting allows insulin levels to decrease, according to Dr. Mitchell Roslin.

2.3 What to Eat and Drink During Intermittent Fasting?

According to Pincus and Purdy, a well-balanced diet is a secret to gaining weight, retaining energy levels, and keeping to the diet.

"Anyone looking to reduce weight should consume nutrient-dense foods like fruits, berries, whole grains, beans, nuts, seeds, dairy, and lean proteins," Pincus advises.

Intermittent fasting has attracted a lot of interest from the current fad diets due to its persuasive experimental proof. Fasting has been a form of political protest, a search for divine fulfillment, and a healing technique throughout history. It's recently gained popularity among exercise gurus due to its claimed weight-loss and anti-aging properties. But that raises the question: Is there an all-encompassing intermittent fasting guide that can tell you what to consume while on this diet?

Let's begin from the beginning and go through the fundamentals: Why does the diet function in terms of intermittent fasting's main health effects? Scientists believe that greater insulin sensitivity is responsible for the anti-aging effects and that weight reduction is linked to a lower average calorie consumption due to a shorter eating window. Simply put, because you don't have too much food to consume throughout the day, you eat less. Isn't it simple? However, as with any diet, deciding viability for your lifestyle is critical.

Diet-induced weight loss, according to a report released in The Lancet Diabetes & Endocrinology, usually results in a 70% weight regain, so the trick is to find a weight-loss diet that fits you and won't hurt you in the future.

Intermittent fasting can be done in various ways, but according to Andres Ayesta, MS, RDN, a licensed dietitian and specialist in the field of fasting, the time-restricted feeding (TRF) procedure is the safest choice for working adults.

"Fasting from 9 p.m. to around 1 p.m. the next day fits great, so most people miss breakfast or eat bad breakfast," says Ayesta. This implies that intermittent fasting, overall diet consistency, and habitual food preferences still matter, and you won't have the body of your dreams from consuming nothing but cheeseburgers and fries. On the IF diet, consuming junk food during a condensed feeding window can put you at risk of deficiency in essential nutrients, including protein, calcium, iron, and fiber, all of which are needed for normal biological function. Besides, a diet abundant in fruits and vegetables helps the body to generate more antioxidants, which, like the physiological benefits of intermittent fasting, can help you live longer.

Here's a rundown of traditional intermittent fasting schedules to get you started:

- Alternate Day Fasting (ADF) consists of one day of ad libitum (normal eating) followed by one day of complete fasting.

- Changed Alternating Day Fasting (CADF)—one day of ad libitum consumption accompanied by one day of a very low-calorie diet (around 24% of normal caloric intake).

- 2/5—2 days of full fasting accompanied by five days of ad libitum feeding.

- 1/6—1 day of complete fasting followed by six days of ad libitum feeding.

- Time Restricting Feeding (TRF)—On each day of the week, easy for 12-20 hours (as a continuation of the nighttime fast). 4-12 hour "feeding time."

1. **Water**

Promoting hydration is one of the most critical ways of sustaining a balanced eating routine during intermittent fasting. After going without food for 12 to 16 hours, our body's natural energy supply is the sugar contained in the liver, also recognized as glycogen. When this energy is used, a substantial amount of fluid and electrolytes are lost. During an intermittent fasting routine, try to drink eight cups of water a day to avoid exhaustion and improve blood pressure, memory, and muscle and joint support.

Yeah, so this isn't a meal, but it's essential for living IF.

Water is essential for the protection of almost all your body's main organs. Avoiding this as part of the diet will be nonsensical. Your lungs play a critical role in keeping you safe.

The amount of water that everyone can drink depends on their gender, height, weight, exercise level, and environment. However, the color of the urine is a strong indicator. At all times, you like it to be pale yellow.

Dehydration, which may induce headaches, nausea, and lightheadedness, is shown by dark yellow urine. If plain water doesn't appeal to you, consider adding a splash of lemon juice, a few fresh mint leaves, or cucumber slices. Here's why H2O reigns supreme.

2. Avocado

Eating the highest-calorie fruit when attempting to lose weight can appear counterintuitive. On the other hand, avocados can help you to remain full through even the most stringent fasting times due to their high unsaturated fat content.

Unsaturated fats, according to research, help hold the body healthy even though you don't feel hungry.

Your body sends out signals that it doesn't need to go into emergency hunger mode because it has enough calories. And if you're starving during a fasting time, unsaturated fats hold these symptoms running much longer.

Another research showed that eating half an avocado with your lunch will help you remain full for hours longer than if you don't consume the green, mushy fruit.

3. Fish and seafood

There's an explanation why the American Dietary Recommendations prescribe two or three 4-ounce portions of fish each week.

In addition to being high in healthier fats and protein, Trusted Source is also high in vitamin D.

And if you like to feed at short window times, don't you want to get more nutritious bang for your buck while you do?

4. Cruciferous veggies

The f-word—fiber—is abundant in foods like brussels sprouts, broccoli, and cauliflower. It's essential to consume fiber-rich foods regularly to keep you regular and ensure that your poop factory runs smoothly.

Fiber will also help you feel whole, which is helpful if you won't feed for another 16 hours.

Cruciferous vegetables will also help you avoid cancer.

5. Potatoes

Repeat after us: White foods aren't all bad.

In the 1990s, researchers discovered that potatoes are one of the most satiating foods.

Besides, a 2012 study showed that using potatoes in a balanced diet can aid weight loss. (Sorry, but potato chips and French fries don't count.) We investigated the association between potato and blood sugar.

6. Beans and legumes

On the IF diet, your favorite chili topping might be your best friend.

Food, especially carbohydrates, provides energy for physical exercise. We're not saying you go nuts with carbohydrates, so having low-calorie carbs like beans and legumes in your diet can't hurt. This will help you stay awake through your fasting period.

Furthermore, ingredients like chickpeas, peas, black beans, and lentils have been proven to help people shed weight, even though they aren't on a diet.

7. Probiotics

What do the tiny critters in your stomach want to feed on the most? Both consistency and variety are essential. If they're starving, this means they're not comfortable. And if your stomach isn't comfortable, you may notice unpleasant side effects, such as constipation.

Add probiotic-rich ingredients to the diet, such as kefir, kombucha, and sauerkraut, to combat this unpleasantness. We spoke to specialists to learn more about how probiotics function in the body.

8. Berries

These smoothie classics are packed with vitamins and minerals. That's not even the most thrilling aspect. People who ate a ton of flavonoids, such as those present in blueberries and strawberries, had lower BMI rises over fourteen years than people who didn't consume berries, according to a 2016 report.

9. Eggs

One big egg has 6.3 grams of protein and takes just minutes to prepare. And, mainly when you're eating less, having quite enough protein as possible is critical for staying full and building muscle.

Men who had an egg breakfast rather than a bagel have been less hungry and ate less during the day, according to a 2010 survey. To put it another way, if you're looking for something else to do during your fast, why not hard-boil a bunch of eggs? And, when the time is perfect, you should consume them.

10. Nuts

While nuts are higher in fat than many other snacks, they do have something that most snacks do not: healthy fats.

According to a 2012 report, a 1-ounce portion of almonds (roughly 23 nuts) provides 20% fewer calories than the label says.

According to the report, chewing does not fully break down the cell walls of almonds, which keeps a part of the nut safe and prevents it from being absorbed by the body through digestion. As a result, eating almonds might not make as much of a difference in your regular calorie intake as you would think.

11. Whole grains

Dieting and carbohydrate intake tends to fall under two distinct groups. This isn't always the case, as you'll be glad to learn. Since whole grains are high in fiber and nutrition, a small amount would keep you satisfied for a long time. So, get out of your comfort zone and try faro, sorghum, spelled, bulgur, amaranth, Kamut, millet, or freekeh, a whole-grain utopia.

12. Coffee

How about a steaming cup of Joe? Can a regular trip to Starbucks be enough to crack the fast? It's a concern so many newbie sporadic fasters have. But don't worry, coffee is permitted. Coffee should legally be drunk outside of a specified eating time since it is a calorie-free product in its natural state.

13. Minimally Processed Grains

Carbohydrates are a natural aspect of life and are not a threat when it comes to reducing weight. Because you'll be fasting for a large portion of the day during this diet, it's critical to plan how you'll get enough calories without feeling bloated. While a balanced diet excludes refined foods, there is a time and place for bagels, whole-grain bread, and crackers, which absorb more efficiently and provide fast and simple energy. These can be a perfect energy source on the go if you want to work out or practice daily during intermittent fasting.

14. Lentils

With 32% of overall regular fiber needs fulfilled in just half a cup, this healthy superstar is a fiber powerhouse. Besides, lentils are a rich source of iron (about 15% of your daily needs), which is another nutrient of concern, particularly for active females who fast intermittently.

15. Seitan

For optimum wellbeing and survival, the EAT-Lancet Commission recently issued a study asking for a significant decrease of animal-based proteins. One major study found a strong correlation between red meat intake and increased mortality. Incorporate life-extending plant-based protein replacements like seitan into your anti-aging diet and get the best bang for your buck. This beef, also recognized as "wheat meat," can be pounded, grilled, and dipped in various sauces.

16. Hummus

Hummus, one of the creamiest and best-tasting dips ever made, is yet another outstanding plant-based protein that can be used to improve the nutritious value of everyday foods like sandwiches by simply substituting it for mayonnaise. If you're bold enough to create your hummus, don't ignore the main ingredients' garlic and tahini.

17. Salmon

If you wish to enter the club of centenarians, you can learn more about the Blue Zones. Dietary and lifestyle preferences related to extreme durability are well established in these five regional regions in Europe, Asia, Latin America, and the United States. Salmon, rich in the brain-boosting omega-3 fatty acids EPA and DHA, is common in these areas.

18. Soybeans

Isoflavone, one of the active ingredients in soybeans, has been shown to prevent UVB-induced cell damage and facilitate anti-aging, as though we wanted another reason to splurge on a sushi bar appetizer. So, the next time you have a dinner party at home, wow your friends with a tasty soybean recipe.

19. Multivitamins

One possible technique for IF induced weight loss is that the person will have less time to eat and thus absorb fewer calories. While a multivitamin isn't needed if you eat a well-balanced variety of fruits and vegetables, life could get hectic, and supplementation can fill in the gaps.

20.   Smoothies

If a daily supplement doesn't sound enticing, consider making organic smoothies with fruits and veggies for a double dose of vitamins. Smoothies are an ideal way to eat a range of ingredients abundant in various vital nutrients.

21. Vitamin D Fortified Milk

A maximum calcium consumption of 1,000 milligrams is suggested for adults, approximately equal to three cups of milk. With a narrower eating time, chances to consume this much can be minimal, so high-calcium foods should be prioritized. Vitamin D fortified milk improves calcium intake and helps to maintain bone strength. You should add the milk to smoothies or cereals, or just drink it with meals, to improve your regular calcium intake. Non-dairy calcium options contain tofu and soy goods, as well as leafy greens like kale if you're not a lover of the soda.

22.   Red Wine

The polyphenol in grapes has distinct anti-aging properties, so a glass of wine and a night of beauty sleep can keep heads turning. SIRT-1 is an enzyme class present in humans believed to function on resveratrol in the face of a caloric deficiency to increase insulin sensitivity and survival.

23.   Papaya

You'll probably start to feel hungry in the final moments of your fast, particularly if you're new to intermittent fasting. This "hanger" can lead to you overeating in large amounts, leaving you exhausted and irritable minutes later. Papain, a unique enzyme found in papaya, acts on proteins to break them down. Incorporating pieces of this tropical fruit into a high-protein meal will aid absorption and reduce bloating.

24.   Nuts

Create space on the cheese board for a mixed selection of nuts since they are believed to help you lose weight and live longer. Nut intake was also linked to a lower incidence of coronary disease, Type 2 diabetes, and total mortality in a prospective trial reported in the British Journal of Nutrition.

25.   Ghee

You've already learned that a drizzle of olive oil has many health benefits, but there are loads of other oil choices to choose from. You don't want to cook with an oil that has reached its smoke point, so the next time you're making a stir-fry, go with ghee. It's essentially clarified butter with a far higher smoke point, making it ideal for hot dishes.

26.   Homemade Salad Dressing

When it applies to salad dressings and sauces, you can follow your grandmother's example and keep things plain. Unwanted ingredients and added sugar are removed as we produce our transparent dressings.

27.   Lean Proteins

According to Maciel, eating lean protein makes you fuller for longer than most diets and helps you sustain or gain strength. Here are five protein sources that are both lean and healthy:

- Breast of chicken

- Greek yogurt, plain

- Lentils, beans, and peas

- Shellfish and fish

- Tempeh and tofu

28.   Fruits

Intermittent fasting, like every other meal plan, necessitates the consumption of high-nutrient foods. Vitamins, phytonutrients (plant nutrients), minerals, and fiber are commonly found in fruits and vegetables. According to the government's 2020-25 Dietary Guidelines for Americans, most citizens can consume around 2 cups of fruit a day on a 2,000-calorie diet.

29.   Vegetables

Vegetables will help you adhere to your intermittent fasting schedule. A diet abundant in leafy greens has been shown to lower the risk of heart failure, Type 2 diabetes, cognitive impairment, cancer, and other diseases. According to the government's 2020-25 Dietary Guidelines for Americans, most individuals can consume 2.5 cups of vegetables a day on a 2,000-calorie diet.

2.4 Intermittent Fasting Myths

Fasting has grown more common in recent years.

Intermittent fasting, a nutritional practice that alternates between fasting and eating times, is often marketed as a miracle diet. However, not everything you've read about the connection between meal frequency and your wellbeing is suitable.

1. Fasting will slow your metabolism down.

If you're afraid or excited at the prospect of slowing your metabolism by intermittent fasting, Blum claims it's a fallacy, and he's here to refute it.

"Intermittent fasting isn't about limiting calories; it's about restricting when calories are eaten," he explained. "There is no difference in metabolic rate if you wait a couple of hours longer to consume your first meal. Undereating causes physiological changes, which do not arise while following an intermittent fasting diet."

2. Fasting is better than snacking for weight loss.

When it comes to dieting, it's common knowledge that you can eat in between meals. One of the most common misconceptions about intermittent fasting is that it be a replacement for balanced snacking.

"A steady calorie imbalance is a key to weight reduction," Blum told INSIDER. "This makes no difference whether such calories are eaten throughout the day or in a four to eight-hour cycle. To meet the objectives you've set, do what's right for your body and lifestyle."

3. You can eat as much as you want when you stop your fast.

Intermittent fasting is just the beginning of a healthy way of life. Unfortunately, many people assume that they will resume their normal eating habits after their fast is over. According to Dr. Mike Roussel, doing so would effectively undo any previous efforts.

"The trick to being effective with I.F. is to eat like you usually will when you split your fast," he clarified. "If you fast all day before dinner and only have a dinner the size of breakfast, lunch, and dinner, the period you spend fasting is negated."

4. Fasting for weight loss works better than other weight-loss strategies.

If you believe that intermittent fasting is the most effective way to lose weight, you might want to reconsider.

"At the most fundamental form, intermittent fasting is a calorie restriction activity," Roussel said. "Intermittent fasting has not been proven to be more successful than other weight-loss approaches."

5. Working out is impossible if you're fasting.

"The perfect opportunity to work out is first thing in the morning with an empty stomach," he told INSIDER. "Instead of burning the calories from what you've already eaten, you'll be burning the fat you've already put on your body. After your exercise, eat breakfast to refill your body."

6. **Eating a big breakfast is a necessity since it's considered the most important meal of the day.**

Though it's common knowledge that you can consume a large breakfast to power your day, Pearlman insists that this isn't always the case.

"The large, full breakfast is a huge part of American culture," he said. "Of course, cereal makers want you to believe it, but you should listen to your body and have a light breakfast (since most people don't have an appetite when they wake up). Then, particularly if you worked out in the morning or missed breakfast completely, you should have a substantial lunch. You have the choice of making every meal your main meal of the day. It's just about figuring out what fits better for your body and lifestyle."

7. **You'll become extremely healthy and fit by fasting.**

Intermittent fasting will help you lose weight when paired with proper treatment and maintenance, but Pearlman warns anyone considering the diet that it is not a secret way to get in shape.

"There is no silver bullet remedy. Don't take your wellbeing and wellness for granted; they are aspects you would struggle to preserve throughout your existence. Fasting won't offer you the perfect body immediately because if you can drop weight, you'll have to keep that off with healthier activities like eating well and exercising regularly."

8. All intermittent fasting is the same, and everyone gets the same results.

Monica Auslander Morena, MS, RD, LD/N, a diet expert for RSP Nutrition, told INSIDER that there are several intermittent fasting methods, contrary to common opinion.

"Intermittent fasting may not have an "approved" meaning. And there is a variety of them. Such I.F. guidelines involve full fasting any single day, while others require eating a fixed number of calories or time-restricted feeding within a six, eight, or ten-hour span regularly."

9. Intermittent fasting presents because your body doesn't deal with foods at night.

The explanation of why fasting functions is a common misunderstanding. Though it's a common misconception that digestion stops after a certain amount of time, Morena told INSIDER that this is not the case.

"No matter what time it is, the body can absorb food," Morena said. "Allowing the body, a significant amount of time (whether experts agree on 12-16-18 hours or not) to concentrate on other biochemical processes including autophagy and cellular repair rather than digestion is the key. And if you feed at 3 a.m., the body can absorb it. To be frank, I'm not a successful choice for I.F. I have a strong Latin late-night dinner plan culture and early morning exercises to pass out if I do not consume breakfast. Besides, if I go to bed too late without sleeping, I am mentally unable to function. Yet here I am, a living and breathing witness."

10. **Eating helps reduce hunger.**

Some people claim that feeding at daily periods helps them reduce cravings and hunger.

However, the proof is contradictory.

While some research suggests that eating more often reduces hunger, others have shown little impact or even elevated hunger levels.

One research showed that consuming three high-protein meals a day decreased hunger more significantly than eating six high-protein meals a day.

Responses, however, can vary depending on the person. It's an intelligent thing to feed if it decreases the cravings. Despite this, there is little proof that feeding more often or snacking decreases appetite in anyone.

Chapter 3: Intermittent Fasting Mistakes That Make You Gain Weight

Intermittent fasting is adequate for most citizens. This eating schedule reduces the number of hours a person consumes per day and has been shown to boost cognitive performance, promote immune health, and aid weight loss.

What if, instead of helping you drop weight, fasting causes you to add weight? Consider whether any of the following seven variables are at work:

1. You must not keep a diary.

If you learn to sustain an intermittent fasting regimen, memorizing what you eat (and don't eat) and monitoring the hours you eat will pay off.

Tracking your food consumption and other measures, such as your regular exercise or mood levels, will help you find possible roadblocks to your progress.

2. You're allowing calories to enter your system during your fasting hours.

Fasting entails consuming no calories—or as few as possible—during your non-eating hours. Specific less-obvious culprits may be interfering with your fast. Even a tiny amount of sweetener or cream in their coffee can cause some people to break their fast.

3. You're consuming too much food.

Fasting will help you control your food consumption without having to count calories. Although they ingested marginally more calories at their next meal than non-fasters, they ingested almost 2,000 extra carbs over the two days, according to one report.

On the other side, breaking a hard fast may sound like an opportunity to eat large quantities of high-calorie food for certain people.

4. You depend on coffee much too much.

A big cup of natural dark roast can be the best introduction to your morning after an overnight fast. Caffeine has the potential to reduce hunger while also increasing energy levels. However, using coffee as a crutch for lousy sleep or mood management can indicate that you're consuming too much, which may lead to weight gain in certain people over time. Caffeine will boost blood glucose levels and extend those changes, making you less insulin-responsive and more prone to store fat, according to some studies.

5. You're consuming the incorrect foods.

Fasting for 18 or even 24 hours doesn't offer you the green light to devour a deep-dish pizza or down a couple bottles of wine during the time you do consume. Those foods and beverages will cause your insulin levels to rise and plunge, taking you on a blood glucose roller coaster that will leave you hungry and irritable during your fasting hours.

It's essential when you eat, but it's also important what you eat. Ensure you're having enough calcium, nutrition, and healthy fats throughout your feeding hours by eating greens, fruits, premium meats and seafood, nuts and seeds, and olive oil.

6. You're traveling way too far, way too fast.

Immediately committing to a 24-hour quick will turn into a complete catastrophe. Instead, begin with a smaller fasting window and work your way up. Experiment with the size of the window and progressively expand it. Don't get off the diving board before you've been used to being in the deeper end.

7. You're not holding to a safe lifestyle.

What you consume and don't eat becomes an integral part of the overall health care plan. Getting at least eight hours of quality sleep every night, controlling tension, sustaining a balanced societal and spiritual life, and eating the best foods to help your fasting attempts and develop excellent health are all equally critical. Fasting gets simpler and has longer-lasting effects as you maintain such healthy practices.

3.1 How to Set Up an Intermittent Fasting Diet?

Intermittent fasting has been a common health practice in recent years. It's said to help people lose weight, boost their metabolic fitness, and maybe even live longer. This eating trend may be approached in a variety of ways. Any strategy can be successful but determining which one works better for you is a personal decision.

Intermittent fasting can be done in six different forms.

1. The 16/8 method

	DAY 1	DAY 2	DAY 3	DAY 4	DAY 5	DAY 6	DAY 7
Midnight							
4 AM	FAST	FAST	FAST	FAST	FAST	FAST	FAST
8 AM							
12 PM	First meal	First meal	First meal	First meal	First meal	First meal	First meal
4 PM	Last meal by 8pm	Last meal by 8pm	Last meal by 8pm	Last meal by 8pm	Last meal by 8pm	Last meal by 8pm	Last meal by 8pm
8 PM / Midnight	FAST	FAST	FAST	FAST	FAST	FAST	FAST

The 16/8 process includes fasting for 14–16 hours a day and limiting your feeding window to 8–10 hours. You may consume two, three, or even four meals during the feeding time. Fitness expert Martin Berkhan popularized this form, which is also known as the Leangains protocol. It's as simple as not consuming something after dinner and missing breakfast to follow this fasting process.

If you have your last meal at 8 p.m. and don't eat again before noon the next day, you'll have fasted for 16 hours. Women are usually advised to fast for just 14–15 hours since they tend to perform well with shorter fasts. This approach can be challenging to adapt to at first for those who are hungry in the morning and like to consume breakfast. Many breakfast-skippers, on the other hand, feed in this manner instinctively.

2. The 5:2 diet

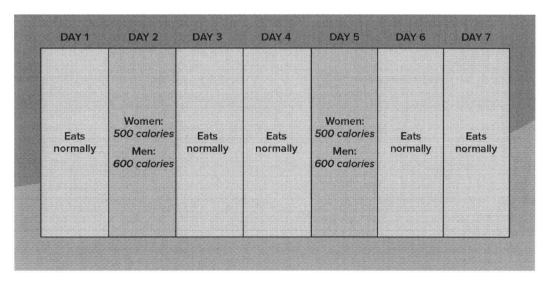

DAY 1	DAY 2	DAY 3	DAY 4	DAY 5	DAY 6	DAY 7
Eats normally	Women: 500 calories Men: 600 calories	Eats normally	Eats normally	Women: 500 calories Men: 600 calories	Eats normally	Eats normally

The 5:2 diet entails regularly eating five days a week and limiting your calorie consumption to 500–600 calories on the other two days. Michael Mosley, a British writer, popularized this diet, which is also regarded as the Easy Diet. On fasting days, women should consume 500 calories, and men should consume 600 calories. You can, for example, regularly eat every day except Mondays and Thursdays.

You consume two small meals of 250 calories each for women and 300 calories each for those two days. No trials evaluate the 5:2 diet itself, as opponents rightly point out, but there are loads of studies about the advantages of intermittent fasting. This diet entails consuming 500–600 calories two days a week and the remaining five days are typically off.

3. Eat Stop Eat

DAY 1	DAY 2	DAY 3	DAY 4	DAY 5	DAY 6	DAY 7
Eats normally	24-hour fast	Eats normally	Eats normally	24-hour fast	Eats normally	Eats normally

Once or twice a week, Eat Stop Eat requires a 24-hour fast.

Fitness specialist Brad Pilon popularized this form, which has been very popular for a few years. This leads to a perfect 24-hour fast if you fast from dinner one day to dinner the next day. You've done a perfect 24-hour fast if you end dinner at 7 p.m. Monday, and don't feed again before dinner at 7 p.m. Tuesday. The result is the same if you fast from breakfast to breakfast, or lunch to lunch.

During the fasting period, liquids such as water, coffee, and other low-calorie drinks are tolerated, but solid foods are not. It would help if you dieted normally during the feeding cycles while you're trying to lose weight. In other words, you can consume as well as you would if you weren't fasting at all.

A complete 24-hour fast can be challenging for certain citizens, which is a possible disadvantage to this approach. You don't have to go all-in right away, however. It's OK to start with 14–16 hours and work your way up.

4. Alternate-day fasting

	DAY 1	DAY 2	DAY 3	DAY 4	DAY 5	DAY 6	DAY 7
	Eats normally	24-hour fast OR Eat only a few hundred calories	Eats normally	24-hour fast OR Eat only a few hundred calories	Eats normally	24-hour fast OR Eat only a few hundred calories	Eats normally

This approach is available in a variety of forms. During fasting days, some may intake around 500 calories. This technique was used in several of the test-tube experiments that demonstrated the health effects of intermittent fasting. A complete fast any other day may seem unnecessary, so it is not suggested for beginners. This approach can cause you to go to bed many hungry days a week, which is inconvenient and unlikely to be sustainable in the long run.

5. The Warrior Diet

	DAY 1	DAY 2	DAY 3	DAY 4	DAY 5	DAY 6	DAY 7
Midnight 4 AM 8 AM 12 PM	Eating only small amounts of vegetables and fruits	Eating only small amounts of vegetables and fruits	Eating only small amounts of vegetables and fruits	Eating only small amounts of vegetables and fruits	Eating only small amounts of vegetables and fruits	Eating only small amounts of vegetables and fruits	Eating only small amounts of vegetables and fruits
4 PM 8 PM Midnight	Large meal	Large meal	Large meal	Large meal	Large meal	Large meal	Large meal

Ori Hofmekler, a lifestyle pioneer, popularized the Warrior Diet. You consume tiny quantities of raw fruits and vegetables during the day, and at night, you eat one large meal. You fast through the day and feed within a four-hour feeding span at night. One of the first standard diets to incorporate a type of intermittent fasting was the Warrior Diet. The food preferences on this diet are somewhat close to those on the paleo diet, consisting entirely of whole, unprocessed ingredients.

6. Spontaneous meal skipping

	DAY 1	DAY 2	DAY 3	DAY 4	DAY 5	DAY 6	DAY 7
	Breakfast	Skipped Meal	Breakfast	Breakfast	Breakfast	Breakfast	Breakfast
	Lunch	Lunch	Lunch	Lunch	Lunch	Lunch	Lunch
	Dinner	Dinner	Dinner	Dinner	Skipped Meal	Dinner	Dinner

You don't have to stick to a strict intermittent fasting schedule to enjoy the advantages. Another choice is to miss meals on occasion, such as when you aren't hungry or when you are too distracted to prepare and eat.

It's a fallacy that people must feed every few hours or risk malnutrition or muscle loss. Your body is designed to withstand long stretches of hunger, let alone missing one or two meals now and then. Therefore, if you're not hungry one day, miss breakfast and have a good lunch and dinner instead. Alternatively, if you're traveling and can't locate something you want to consume, go on a quick fast. A random sporadic fast is when you skip one or two meals when you feel like it. During the other meals, make sure you consume nutritious snacks.

3.2 The Dangers of Intermittent Fasting

In the field of nutrition, intermittent fasting seems to be all the rage these days. Intermittent fasting, on the other hand, is not a novel phenomenon. Indeed, people have fasted throughout history for a variety of causes ranging from religious to nutritional shortages. Intermittent fasting—and the evidence that supports it—has only lately captured the eye of the public as a great way to diet and lose weight.

"Evidence is emerging that eating in a 6-hour cycle and fasting for 18 hours will cause a metabolic transition from glucose-based to ketone-based capacity, with improved stress tolerance, increased survival, and a decreased occurrence of dis-ease," writers Rafael de Cabo, Ph.D., and Mark P. Mattson, Ph.D., wrote in a broad analysis published in the December 2019 issue of the New England Journal of Medicine.

Several experiments have discovered that such fasting regimens will shield animals from cognitive loss, diabetes, and cardiac disease. Intermittent fasting has also been found to reduce cancer and delay the aging process. However, the consequences of intermittent fasting—beyond weight loss—have primarily been studied in cellular and animal experiments, and the effects on humans have yet to be determined.

According to preliminary findings from a few clinical studies, some fasting forms can help with glucose regulation, blood pressure reduction, and inflammation reduction. Researchers are yet to determine if these benefits are related to fasting or weight loss since fasting induces weight loss.

Intermittent fasting, like anything else, has its drawbacks. Whether you're thinking of doing intermittent fasting or already do so, keep in mind that it has certain disadvantages. Here are a few that you should be conscious of:

Orthorexia is a condition in which an individual is unable. Intermittent fasting has been related to eating disorders like orthorexia, which is described as a fixation with correct or "good" eating. Symptoms show a persistent desire to discuss your food and an obsession about what you will consume next. If you find that your lifestyle has been rigid, to the point that you skip or postpone social activities because they conflict with your eating patterns, pay attention, and try transitioning to a different diet.

Sleep deprivation. While not eating before bedtime increases sleep capacity, intermittent fasting has been found to interrupt your sleep cycle by reducing the amount of REM sleep you receive. Memory, temperament, and learning ability all gain from REM sleep.

Reduced vigilance. Although intermittent fasting has been shown to improve alertness, it has also been shown to decrease it over time. This is essentially attributed to the body not receiving enough fuel and being unable to produce sufficient electricity. Fasting can trigger nausea, concentration problems, and even dizziness.

Guilt has increased. Eating too early or too late will trigger anxiety and embarrassment if you break your fast or miss your fasting time. Keep on the lookout for these thoughts since they could signify something more sinister, such as disordered feeding.

Cortisol levels have risen. Fasting puts a strain on the body, which may raise cortisol levels, mainly if you go without food for an extended period. Cortisol is the body's stress hormone, and higher levels have been linked to stress and fat accumulation.

LDL cholesterol levels are higher. Researchers discovered substantially higher LDL amounts by month 12 in metabolically stable obese individuals who did alternate-day fasting in one randomized clinical study relative to others who did normal calorie limits.

Harm to the pancreas. Brazilian researchers discovered that after a 90-day alternate-day fasting diet, lab rats lost weight but added muscle and abdominal fat, according to a report presented at the European Society of Endocrinology's annual meeting in 2018. Furthermore, variations in the pancreas indicated an increased likelihood of diabetes.

Even though studies appear to be making progress, the long-term consequences of intermittent fasting remain uncertain. If you're worried about integrating intermittent fasting into your routine, or if your patients ask for your guidance, bear this in mind. And, whether you're planning to observe or advocate intermittent fasting, also bear in mind that it can be achieved in a convenient and balanced manner.

3.3 Types of Intermittent Fasting

There are various ways to do IF, which is fantastic. If this is something you're involved in, you may pick the form that better fits your needs, improving the likelihood of success. Here are seven of them:

1. 5:2 Fasting

This is one of the most often used IF techniques. The book The Fast Diet popularized it and explained everything you need to know about it. The plan is to diet regularly for five days (without measuring calories) and then ingest 500 or 600 calories a day for women and men, respectively, for the remaining two days. The fasting days can be any days you like.

The writers of The Fast Diet, though, warn against fasting for days where you're performing a lot of endurance exercise. If you're practicing for a cycling or running ride (or a high-mileage week), visit a sports nutritionist to see if this form of fasting can fit with your training schedule.

2. Time-Restricted Fasting

This form of IF allows you to choose an eating window per day, which should leave you with a 14 to 16 hour fast. (Shemek advises women to fast for no longer than 14 hours a day due to hormonal concerns.) "Fasting encourages autophagy, the body's normal 'cellular housekeeping' mechanism that starts when liver glycogen is exhausted and clears debris and other items that get in the way of mitochondrial health," Shemek says. According to her, doing so can significantly boost fat cell metabolism and optimize insulin function.

Set the meal window, for example, from 9 a.m. to 5 p.m. to make this work. According to Kumar, this fits well for anyone who has a family that eats an early dinner anyway. And there's the reality that most of the time spent fasting is spent dreaming. (Depending on where you scheduled your window, you still don't have to "skip" any meals.) However, this is contingent on the ability to remain consistent. Regular times of fasting might not be for you if your life is constantly shifting, or if you need and want the freedom to go out to brunch on occasion, go on a late date night, or go to happy hour.

3. Overnight Fasting

This form is the most basic of them all, including fasting for 12 hours a day. Consider the following scenario: Choose to avoid feeding around 7 p.m. after dinner and start eating at 7 a.m. the following day with tea. At the 12-hour point, autophagy also exists, but the cellular benefits are milder, according to Shemek. This is the bare minimum of fasting hours she advises.

This approach has the benefit of being quick to execute. You don't have to miss meals; what you're doing is cutting out a bedtime snack (if you ate one, to begin with). However, this approach would not fully exploit the benefits of fasting. If you're fasting to lose weight, a narrower fasting window ensures you'll have more food to feed and does not make you ingest fewer calories.

4. Eat Stop Eat

You agree to a resistance exercise regimen and one or two 24-hour fasts per week.

Eating means adjusting to a regular eating schedule in which you don't indulge when you've already fasted, but you still don't deprive yourself or consume less than you require. Fat reduction is better accomplished by mixing extended fasting with routine weightlifting, according to Pilon. You will consume a marginally more significant number of calories on the other five to six non-fasting days, whether you go on one of two 24-hour fasts throughout the week. He claims that this allows a smoother and more fun finish to the week in a calorie shortage without feeling compelled to go on a strict diet.

5. Whole-Day Fasting

You just feed once a day here. According to Shemek, certain people prefer to consume dinner and then not eat again before the next day's dinner. That means you'll be fasting for 24 hours. This is not the same as the 5:2 form. Fasting times are usually 24 hours, while 5:2 includes a 36-hour fast. (For example, you could eat dinner on Sunday, then go on a 500-600 calorie fast on Monday before breaking it with breakfast on Tuesday.)

The benefit is that, if achieved for weight reduction, eating a whole day's worth of calories in one sitting is very difficult (though not impossible). The downside of this strategy is that it's tough to provide all the nutrition your body needs with only one meal. Not to mention, sticking to this strategy is challenging. By the time dinner comes, you may feel ravenous, causing you to eat less-than-healthy, calorie-dense items. Consider this: When you're hungry, broccoli isn't the first thing that comes to mind. According to Shemek, often people consume too much coffee to satisfy their appetite, which may disrupt their sleep. If you don't feed, you can experience brain fog during the day.

6. Alternate-Day Fasting

People can fast every other day, comprising 25% of their daily calorie requirements (approximately 500 calories) and non-fasting days being regular eating days. This is a common weight-loss technique. Dr. Varady and colleagues observed that alternate day fasting successfully helped obese adults lose weight in a limited study reported in Nutrition Journal. By week two, the participants' side effects (such as hunger) had subsided, and by week four, they were becoming more satisfied with the diet.

Chapter 4: Intermittent Fasting for Women over 50

You won't have to deprive yourself if you practice intermittent fasting, also known as IF. It also doesn't grant you permission to eat a bunch of fatty food while you aren't fasting. Instead of consuming meals and treats during the day, you feed over a set period.

Most citizens stick to an IF plan that allows them to fast for 12 to 16 hours a day. They enjoy regular meals and treats most of the day. Since most people sleep for around eight hours during their fasting hours, sticking to this feeding window isn't as difficult as it seems. You're often advised to consume zero-calorie beverages like wine, tea, and coffee.

For the strongest intermittent fasting outcomes, build an eating routine that fits you. Include the following example:

- 12-hour fasts: A 12-hour sprint entails skipping breakfast and waiting for lunch to feed. You might eat an early supper and skip evening snacks if you want to eat your morning lunch. A 12-12 fast is relatively simple to maintain for older women.

- 16-hour fasts: A 16-8 IF schedule will help you achieve faster performance. Within 8 hours, most people prefer to eat two meals and a snack or two. For example, the eating window may be fixed between noon and 8 p.m., or between 8 a.m. and 4 p.m.

- 5-2 timetable: Limited feeding times may not be ideal for you regularly. Another choice is to follow a 12- or 16-hour fast for five days and then rest for two days. For example, you might do intermittent fasting throughout the week and eat regularly on the weekends.

- Alternate-day fasts: Another choice is to consume minimal calories on alternate days. For starters, you might limit your calories to under 500 calories one day and then eat normally the next. It's worth noting that regular IF fasts never necessitate calorie restrictions that low.

You'll have the most potent effects from this diet if you stick to it. Around the same period, you should certainly take a break from this kind of eating routine on rare days. It would help if you tried different intermittent fasting types to see which one is suitable for you. Many people begin their IF journey with the 12-12 plan and then move to the 16-8 plan. After that, strive to adhere to the schedule as near as possible.

According to some facts, intermittent fasting might not be as effective for some women as it is for men. One research noticed that after three weeks of extended fasting, women's blood sugar management deteriorated, while men's did not.

There have also been several observational accounts about women's menstrual cycles shifting since they started intermittent fasting. Since female bodies are particularly vulnerable to calorie restriction, such changes are subject to arise.

A small portion of the brain called the hypothalamus is impaired when calorie consumption is limited, such as when fasting for too long or too often.

The excretion of gonadotropin-releasing hormone (GnRH) is a hormone that aids in the excretion of two reproductive hormones FSH and LH, which may be disrupted because of this.

When these hormones cannot interact with the ovaries, irregular cycles, miscarriage, poor bone strength, and other health problems may occur.

While no analogous human trials exist, experiments in rats have shown that alternate-day fasting for 3–6 months reduced ovary size and triggered erratic reproductive cycles in female rats.

Women should expect a changed solution to intermittent fasting, such as shorter fasting times and fewer fasting days, because of these variables.

4.1 Impact of Aging on Overall Health of Women

These are some of the metabolic modifications that IF induces, which can further understand the synergistic effects:

- Insulin: Lower insulin levels during the fasting cycle will aid fat burning.

- Human Growth Hormone (HGH): As insulin levels decline, HGH levels increase, encouraging fat burning and muscle growth.

53

- Noradrenaline: When your stomach is empty, your nervous system sends this chemical to your cells to tell them they need to produce fat for food.

- Is intermittent fasting a healthy way to eat? Know that you can just sprint for 12 to 16 hours at a time, not for days. You still have plenty of time to eat a delicious and nutritious meal. Of course, certain older women may need regular feeding due to metabolic diseases or drug guidance. Under any scenario, you can speak to the doctor about your dietary patterns before making any adjustments.

- Although it's not fasting, some physicians say that allowing easy-to-digest foods like fruit during the fasting time has health benefits. Modifications like this will also offer a much-needed break for the digestive and metabolic processes. e.g., the famous weight-loss book "Fit for Life" recommended consuming just fruit after supper and before lunch.

- Intermittent fasting tends to offer a broad variety of health effects. The tossing of a metabolic shift may potentially cause these results.

- "Fasting causes glucose [blood sugar] levels to drop. Since transforming fat into ketones, the body utilizes fat instead of glucose as a source of energy," Kathy McManus, head of the Department of Nutrition at the Harvard-affiliated Brigham and Women's Hospital, says. The transition from glucose to ketones as an energy source has a beneficial effect on body chemistry.

- Animals who fast regularly lose weight, have lower blood pressure and heart rates, have low insulin resistance, have lower "poor" LDL cholesterol levels, higher "healthy" HDL cholesterol levels, and have less inflammation. Improved memory has also been discovered in several trials.

- At least in livestock, prolonged fasting is related to a longer lifespan. What is the reason for this? According to a recent Harvard study, intermittent fasting can enable each cell's energy-producing engines (mitochondria) to generate energy more efficiently and sustain a more youthful state.

- "When feeding during the day, you're not challenging the mitochondria at night because they're meant to be doing other stuff," says Dr. William Mair, a Harvard T.H. Chan School of Public Health researcher and associate professor of genetics and complex diseases. "However, we also have a lot of unanswered questions."

4.2 Health Benefits of Intermittent Fasting for Women

Intermittent fasting will help you shed weight while still lowering the risk of contracting a host of chronic diseases.

Heart disease is the primary cause of death in the country.

High blood pressure, high LDL cholesterol, and high triglyceride levels are three of the most critical risk factors for cardiac failure. Intermittent fasting decreased blood pressure by 6% in only eight weeks in a sample of 16 obese men and women.

According to the same report, intermittent fasting also reduced LDL cholesterol by 25% and triglycerides by 32%. The evidence for a correlation between intermittent fasting and lower LDL cholesterol and triglyceride levels, on the other hand, is mixed.

Four weeks of intermittent fasting over the Islamic holiday of Ramadan did not result in a decrease in LDL cholesterol or triglycerides, according to a survey of 40 normal-weight individuals. Until researchers comprehend entirely the impact of intermittent fasting on cardiac health, more excellent studies with more rigorous methods are needed.

1. Diabetes

Intermittent fasting will also help you control your diabetes and decrease your chance of contracting it. Intermittent fasting, including prolonged calorie restriction, tends to reduce some diabetes risk factors.

It mainly accomplishes this by reducing insulin levels and decreasing insulin tolerance.

Six months of intermittent fasting cut insulin levels by 29% and insulin tolerance by 19% in a randomized controlled trial of more than 100 overweight or obese women. The blood sugar levels stayed unchanged.

Furthermore, intermittent fasting for 8–12 weeks has been found to decrease insulin levels by 20–31% and blood sugar levels by 3–6% in people with pre-diabetes, a disorder in which blood sugar levels are typical but not elevated enough to diagnose diabetes.

In terms of blood sugar, though, intermittent fasting might not be as effective for women as men. A small study showed that women's blood sugar management deteriorated after 22 days of alternate day fasting, although men's blood sugar levels remained unchanged.

Given this side effect, the decrease in insulin and insulin tolerance will reduce the incidence of diabetes, particularly in pre-diabetic individuals.

2. Weight Loss

When performed correctly, intermittent fasting can be an easy and efficient way to reduce weight since brief fasts can help you eat fewer calories.

Several reports have found that intermittent fasting is just as successful as conventional calorie-restricted diets for weight loss in the short term. Intermittent fasting resulted in an overall weight reduction of 15 lbs. (6.8 kg) over 3–12 months, according to a 2018 study of research in overweight adults.

According to another study, over 3–24 weeks, intermittent fasting decreased body weight by 3–8% in overweight or obese individuals. According to the report, participants lowered their waist circumference by 3–7% during the same period. It's worth remembering that the long-term consequences of intermittent fasting on female weight loss are also unclear.

Intermittent fasting seems to help with weight reduction in the short term. However, the amount you lose can most definitely be determined by how many calories you eat during non-fasting hours and how long you stick to the lifestyle.

3. It May Help You Eat Less

Switching to intermittent fasting may help you eat less naturally. According to one report, when young men's food consumption was limited to a four-hour duration, they consumed 650 fewer calories per day.

Another research looked at the impact of a lengthy, 36-hour fast on 24 active men and women's eating behaviors. Despite eating more calories on the post-fast day, participants' overall calorie balance fell by 1,900 calories, a substantial decrease.

4. Reduced inflammation

Intermittent fasting has been shown in several experiments to suppress essential markers of inflammation. Chronic inflammation can trigger weight gain and a slew of other health issues.

5. Improved Psychological Well-being

In one report, eight weeks of intermittent fasting lowered stress and binge eating habits in obese adults while also enhancing body appearance.

6. Increased Longevity

Intermittent fasting was shown to having an extra lifespan of 33–83% in rats and mice. The effect on human survival is yet to be calculated.

7. Preserve Muscle Mass

As opposed to prolonged calorie restriction, intermittent fasting tends to be more efficient at sustaining muscle mass. And when you're at rest, getting more muscle mass makes you eat more calories.

4.3 Best Types of Intermittent Fasting for Women

Women can, on average, take a more casual approach to fasting than men.

Shorter fasting times, fewer fasting days, and eating a limited number of calories on fasting days are all potential choices.

Here are a few of the better intermittent fasting options for women:

- Crescendo Method: Fasting for 12–16 hours twice a week for two or three days. Fasting days should not be sequential and should be spread out uniformly throughout the week (e.g., Monday, Wednesday, and Friday).

- The eat-stop-eat rule (also known as the 24-hour protocol): Once or twice a week, go on a complete 24-hour fast (maximum of 2 times a week for women). Start with 14–16 hour fasts and work your way up.

- The 5:2 Diet (also known as "The Quick Diet"): Limit calories to 25% of your daily consumption (about 500 calories) for two days a week and eat "normally" for the other five days. Fasting days can be separated by one day.

- Changed Alternate-Day Fasting: Fasting on alternate days but regularly consuming on non-fasting days. You are permitted to eat 20–25% of your daily calorie intake (roughly 500 calories).

- The 16/8 Method (also known as the "Leangains approach"): Involves fasting for 16 hours a day and consuming all the calories within eight hours. Women can begin with 14-hour fasts and work their way up to 16 hours.

It is also necessary to eat well throughout the non-fasting times, regardless of which alternative you chose. You do not experience the same weight reduction and health effects if you consume tons of fatty, calorie-dense items during the non-fasting times.

At the last stage of the day, the right strategy is something that you can handle and retain over time without having any detrimental health effects.

4.4 A Boon or A Curse for Women?

Intermittent fasting isn't for everybody. The most known side effect of intermittent fasting is hunger. You can also experience weakness, dizziness, and a loss of focus. These would only be temporary since the body may require time to adjust to the new meal plan. Before attempting intermittent fasting, contact the doctor if you have a medical problem. If you have diabetes, this is especially necessary.

- You're having trouble controlling your blood sugar.

- You have a low blood pressure level.

- Take your medicine as prescribed.

- You're overweight.

- Also had an eating problem in the past.

- You are planning to conceive.

- You have a diagnosis of amenorrhea.

- You are pregnant or breastfeeding.

Should Women Fast?

According to some data, intermittent fasting might not be as effective for women as it is for men. One research reported that it increased insulin sensitivity in men but worsened blood sugar regulation in women. Despite the lack of human research on the topic, studies in rats have shown that intermittent fasting causes female rats to become emaciated, masculinized, and infertile, as well as skip periods. Women can avoid strict intermittent fasting because of these factors.

While you're at it, what kind of meals do you eat? Even though intermittent fasting does not dictate which foods to consume, you can eat a nutritious diet that restricts or excludes junk and fatty foods. When you eat fatty foods, you will gain weight and develop diseases.

Concentrate on consuming a well-balanced diet high in fruits, lean proteins, vegetables, whole grains, and good fats (from olives, fish, coconut, avocado, etc.). A diet rich in fiber will leave you feeling complete and happy for longer. Drinking plenty of water is particularly necessary while you're fasting since it assists in satiating hunger, as thirst is sometimes mistaken for hunger.

4.5 Intermittent Is Just Not A Weight Loss Method- It Is A Holistic Health Concept

Diet plays a vital part in preserving and strengthening one's fitness, as we all know. Besides, various foods can be used to enhance one's wellness. So, which diet plan is the most effective? Ok, that depends on various things such as the individual's height and weight, the kind of food they like eating, their degree of fitness, and so on. However, of the many options accessible, intermittent fasting has become increasingly common, particularly in recent years. Some may dismiss it as a fad, but it is a tried-and-true approach backed by empirical study and trials.

Intermittent fasting is based on eating for a fixed period per day and only eating calories for the day's remainder. There are two approaches to do this in general. The first is a regular time-restricted feeding process, in which the person has a 6-8 hour eating window every day, and the second is a 5:2 sporadic fast. The 5:2 strategy entails limiting one's intake to one moderately sized meal twice a week.

It is entirely up to you to decide which form to use. However, the science behind both is somewhat similar. At the most superficial level, intermittent fasting is used to control the body's insulin response. Insulin is a hormone that regulates a variety of functions in the body, including energy absorption and fat accumulation.

Our current objective is to maintain insulin going while we want it to. We can better improve energy intake and fat burning by varying the periods that our insulin levels spike. Since our bodies' insulin production is inadequate during fasting, fat accumulation is prevented, and fat is now burned and used as food. When we eat right after a fast, on the other side, the increase in insulin is robust, which is then used for improved energy intake from the food we eat.

Intermittent fasting has also been shown in experiments to better increase cellular wellbeing by a mechanism known as metabolic switching. This procedure, like the previous one, burns fat and can significantly boost one's wellbeing. It has been shown to help with blood sugar control, stress tolerance, and inflammation suppression.

Weight reduction is another clear outcome of these methods. Individuals will lose the required amount of weight to resolve obesity-related concerns when fat burning is prioritized. A study at the University Hospital of South Manchester found that people who followed an intermittent fasting plan lost the same amount of weight as those who followed a daily calorie-restricted diet. Furthermore, those who followed an extended fasting regimen had higher insulin response and less belly fat.

Intermittent fasting has recently been found to be helpful to brain wellbeing in research. Via a series of cognitive assessments, participants in an intermittent fasting regimen with limited calories showed increased memory in a clinical study at the University of Toronto. More evidence is needed to back up these assertions and further appreciate their brain development effect, but the signals are all pointing to promising outcomes.

As you can see, there are many advantages of using an extended fasting technique. Intermittent fasting can be the secret to optimizing every individual's overall wellbeing, from physical to mental health. Intermittent fasting is a healthy and prosperous technique that is supported by evidence.

Chapter 5: Key Chronic Health Issues Women Face After 50

Although men and women often fall ill, specific health problems impact women differently and more often. Furthermore, many women's health problems go undiagnosed, and several vaccine studies exclude women from participation. Despite this, women experience specific health challenges, including cervical cancer, breast cancer, menopause, and maternity. Women die from cardiac problems at a greater rate than males. Female patients are more likely to experience depression and anxiety. Females are more prone to develop urinary tract infections, and sexually transmitted illnesses may be more dangerous. The following eight diseases are among the most common in women and are associated with significant health threats.

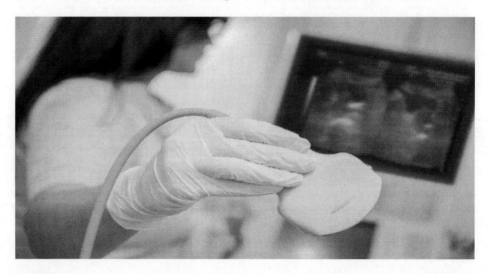

5.1 Heart Disease

Heart attacks kill one out of every four women in the United States. While heart failure is generally identified with males, it affects both men and women in approximately equal numbers. Despite this, only 54% of women are aware that heart failure is the leading cause of women's death. In the United States, 49% of customers have elevated blood pressure, higher levels of cholesterol, or smoke, all of which are risk factors for heart failure.

5.2 Breast Cancer

Breast cancer, which begins in covering the milk ducts and may spread to other tissues, is the most severe cancer that affects women worldwide. Because of their longer life spans, the disease impacts many women in developing countries.

One of the early signs of breast cancer in patients is lumps in their breasts. While most breast lumps are harmless, women need to get each one examined by a healthcare professional.

5.3 Ovarian and Cervical Cancer

Most individuals remain concerned with the variations between ovarian and cervical cancers. Ovarian cancer begins in the fallopian tubes, while cervical cancer begins in the lower uterus. Cervical cancer causes discharge and discomfort during sex, close to the pain caused by both diseases.

Although the signs of ovarian cancer are exceedingly ambiguous, the disease is complicated. Finally, although Pap smears diagnose cervical cancer, they do not detect ovarian cancer.

5.4 Gynaecological Health

The menstrual cycle includes periods of bleeding and discharge. Added signs during menstruation can suggest a health problem, and irregular symptoms, such as blood between periods and excessive urination, may be mistaken for other illnesses.

Vaginal symptoms may be a symptom of a more severe issue, such as sexually transmitted infections (STIs) or cancer of the reproductive tract. Although mild infections can be quickly treated, they may contribute to complications such as infertility or kidney failure if left untreated.

5.5 Pregnancy Issues

Pre-existing conditions will intensify during breastfeeding, placing a mother and her child's health at risk. If asthma, diabetes, or depression are not treated adequately during pregnancy, they may affect both the mother and the infant.

Pregnancy may trigger a stable mother's red blood cell count to decrease, resulting in anemia or making her depressed. Another concern exists as a reproductive cell insert beyond the uterus, stopping future pregnancy. On the other hand, obstetricians can handle and treat both typical and uncommon health problems during pregnancy.

5.6 Autoimmune Diseases

When body cells that generally kill hazards such as viruses invade healthy cells, this is an autoimmune disorder. It puzzles researchers as to why this disease mainly impacts women, as it tends to spread among the population. While there are several autoimmune disorders, they all have symptoms in common, such as exhaustion, mild fever, pain, skin inflammation, and vertigo.

The stomach houses most of the inflammatory disease. As a result, many people who suffer from this disease have turned to natural healing methods like eating less food, eating less fat, lowering tension, and reducing toxin consumption. Early diagnosis, on the other hand, is the most robust protection against autoimmune disorders.

5.7 Osteoporosis

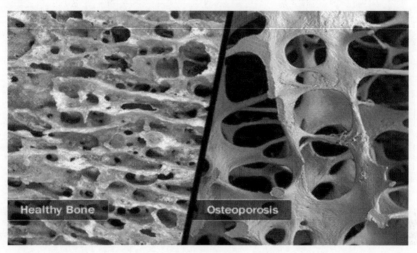

Osteoporosis weakens muscles, making them more likely to crack. Age, alcohol intake, some medications, genetics, lack of activity, low body fat, smoking, and steroid usage are also possible causes of the disease, affecting predominantly women.

Bone density is calculated using an X-ray or ultrasound diagnostic to diagnose the disease. Although there is no remedy for osteoporosis, physicians may recommend treatment to slow down the disease's development, such as nutritional pills, healthier lifestyle improvements, or prescription drugs.

5.8 Depression and Anxiety

Normal hormone variations may trigger depression and anxiety. Premenstrual syndrome (PMS) is a widespread ailment in women, although premenstrual dysmorphic disorder (PMDD) has identical but much more severe signs. Many mothers experience the "baby blues" shortly after giving birth, but perinatal depression triggers related—but often more severe—issues, mood swings, sadness, and exhaustion. Perimenopause, or the change from menopause to perimenopause, may be depressing. Depression is among the most prevalent psychiatric illnesses for people aged 18 and up in the United States. When health issues emerge, loved ones pass away or move away, and other life changes occur, certain people get sad.

5.9 Obesity

Obesity is described as weighing significantly more than is healthy for your height; it is not just gaining a few extra pounds. At least 20 chronic illnesses have been related to it, including coronary failure, stroke, cancer, diabetes, high blood pressure, and arthritis. Obesity impacts almost half of all Americans aged 40 to 59.

5.10 Diabetes

Diabetes affects around one out of every ten people in the United States. As you grow older, the odds of contracting the disease increase. Diabetes may cause heart failure, kidney disease, blindness, and a variety of other complications. Have an appointment with your doctor to get your blood sugar tested.

5.11 High blood pressure

Your blood vessels get less functional as you mature, placing strain on the mechanism that transfers blood across the body. That may clarify why almost two-thirds of adults over the age of 60 have elevated blood pressure. Other factors, though, remain beyond your influence. To avoid it, maintain track of your weight, work out, avoid smoking, learn to cope with tension, and eat well.

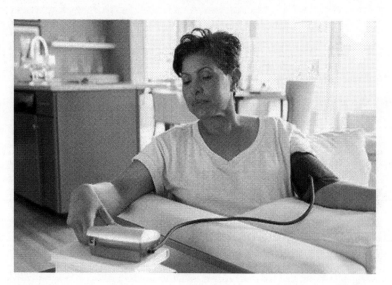

5.12 Cardiovascular diseases

Heart damage is caused by plaque accumulation in the arteries. It begins in infancy and worsens when you grow older. In the United States, 6.3% of men and 5.6% of women in the 40-to-59 age range had heart failure. Heart disorder impacts about 20% of men and 9.7% of women between the ages of 60 and 79.

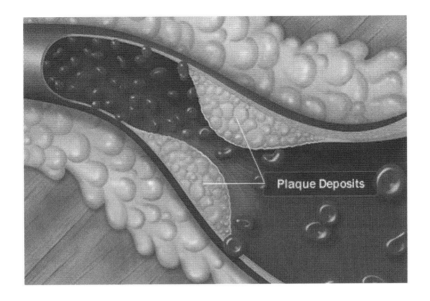

5.13 Osteoarthritis

Doctors used to attribute joint disease to the wear and tear of age, which is still a consideration. However, biology and lifestyle influences are likely to play a part. Previous joint problems, a lack of physical exercise, asthma, and obesity may all play a role.

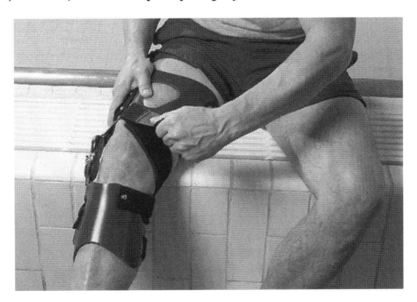

5.14 Chronic Obstructive Pulmonary Disease (COPD)

This results in inflammation which prevents oxygen from entering the lungs. It's a slow-moving illness that may go untreated for years; signs usually start in the 40s or 50s. It can make you cough, wheeze, vomit up mucus, and it can make you have difficulty breathing. Exercising, eating a balanced diet, and staying away from smoke and pollution will all improve these symptoms.

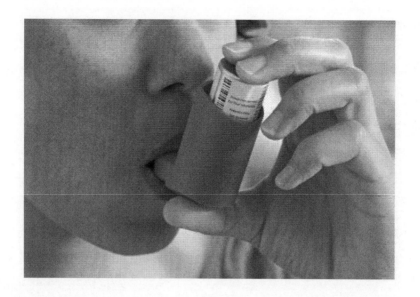

5.15 Hearing Loss

Nothing else means "You're growing older," like needing to enquire, "What did you say?" Hearing damage that is "disabling" impacts around 2% of Americans aged 45 to 54. For those aged 55 to 64, the percentage rises to 8.5%. Loud motion, illness, and genes are both factors. Specific prescriptions may often cause hearing issues. If you can't hear as clearly as you used to, see the doctor.

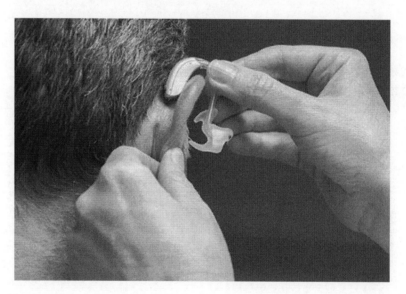

5.16 Vision Problems

The irritating blurriness you get when trying to decipher tiny print on labels or menus isn't the only danger to your eyesight as you get older. Your eyesight may be harmed by cataracts (clouding the lens of your eye) and glaucoma (a category of eye disorders that affect the optic nerve). Examine your eyes daily and occasionally with your eye specialist.

5.17 Cancer

The most critical risk factor for cancer is one's age. The illness also impacts young people, but your risk of catching it more than double between 45 and 54. You have little power over your age or your chromosomes, but you do have control over factors like alcohol and overexposure to the light.

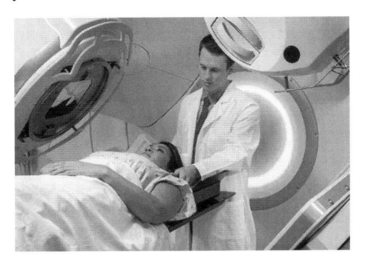

5.18 Back Pain

This is more popular as you grow older. Being overweight, smoking, not having enough exercise, or illnesses like arthritis and cancer will also increase the chances of getting it. To keep your bones healthy, keep track of your weight, work out, and eat lots of vitamin D and calcium. Often, please focus on the back muscles; you'll need them.

5.19 Dementia

Alzheimer's disease, a type of dementia, commonly strikes people over the age of 65. Any risk factors (such as age and heredity) are uncontrollable. However, research shows that maintaining a heart-healthy diet and keeping a careful eye on blood pressure and blood sugar levels can benefit.

Chapter 6: Burning Fat with Intermittent Fasting

6.1 Fat-Burning and Weight Loss

Burning off extra fat can be difficult, whether you're trying to better your general fitness or trim down for the season. Numerous other causes, in addition to diet and exercise, may affect weight and fat loss. Fortunately, there are several easy measures you may follow to improve fat burning rapidly and reliably. Below are 14 of the most successful fat-burning and weight-loss methods.

1. Start Strength Training

Strength training is an activity in which you tense your muscles against resistance. It helps to improve muscle mass and power. Physical exercise is most often correlated with raising weights to develop body density over time. Strength training has been shown to have various health benefits, especially when it comes to fat burning.

Strength exercise was shown to reduce abdominal fat in 78 people with metabolic syndrome in one research. Visceral fat is a harmful form of fat that encircles the organs in the abdomen. Another research found that 12 weeks of resistance training combined with aerobic exercise was more successful than aerobic exercise alone at lowering body fat and belly fat.

Resistance training can also help you maintain fat-free mass, which will help you eat more calories at rest. According to one study, ten weeks of resistance training can help you burn 7% more calories at rest while also losing 4 pounds of fat (1.8 kg). Bodyweight drills, raising weights, and utilizing workout facilities are only a couple of the simple ways to begin strength training.

2. Follow a High-Protein Diet

Increasing the number of protein-rich foods in your diet will help you lose weight and reduce your appetite. Consuming more high-quality protein has been linked to a lower risk of belly fat in multiple studies.

A high-protein diet can also help build muscle and metabolism during weight loss, according to one report. Raising your protein consumption will help you lose weight by increasing sensations of fullness, reducing appetite, and lowering calorie intake.

To further boost fat burning, have a few portions of high-protein foods in your daily diet. Meat, fish, eggs, legumes, and dairy goods are examples of protein-rich foods.

3. Squeeze in More Sleep

Going to bed early or setting your alarm clock later will help you burn more calories and stop adding weight. A connection between having enough sleep and weight loss has been discovered in several studies. Over 16 years, a survey of 68,183 people reported that those who slept for five or fewer hours per night were more likely to become overweight than those who slept for more than seven hours a night.

Another research found that getting at least seven hours of sleep a night and an improved sleep quality raised the chances of good weight loss by 33% in 245 women participating in a 6-month weight loss program.

According to other studies, a lack of sleep may lead to changes in hunger hormones, increased appetite, and an increased risk of obesity. While everybody requires varying amounts of sleep, several researchers have discovered that having at least 7 hours of sleep a night is linked to the most significant weight loss benefits. To promote a healthier sleep period, stick to a daily sleep routine, restrict your caffeine consumption, and limit your mobile device usage before bed.

4. Add Vinegar to Your Diet

Vinegar is well-known for its health-beneficial qualities.

According to some studies, raising your vinegar intake may help improve fat burning, in addition to its possible effects on heart health and blood sugar regulation.

Throughout a 12-week cycle, one research showed that drinking 1–2 tablespoons (15–30 ml) of vinegar every day decreased people's body weight, belly fat, and average waist circumference.

Vinegar consumption has also been found to increase feelings of fullness and decrease appetite. A small sample of 11 participants reported that integrating vinegar into one's diet decreased total calorie consumption by up to 275 calories.

Vinegar is simple to add to your diet. For example, many individuals dilute apple cider vinegar with water and consume it as a cocktail with meals a couple of times a day. If drinking vinegar straight doesn't appeal to you, you can make dressings, sauces, and marinades with it.

5. Eat More Healthy Fats

Increasing your consumption of healthy fats, even though it might seem counterintuitive, may help you avoid weight gain and retain feelings of fullness. Fat takes a long time to absorb and can delay stomach emptying, which can help suppress appetite and hunger. When opposed to a low-fat diet, a Mediterranean diet rich in good fats from olive oil and nuts was linked to a lower risk of weight gain, according to one report.

Another research discovered that people who ate two tablespoons (30 ml) of coconut oil daily on a weight-loss diet shed more belly fat than those who consumed soybean oil. Meanwhile, in human and animal research, unhealthy fats, including Trans-fats, have raised body weight, waist circumference, and belly fat.

Olive oil, avocados, coconut oil, almonds, and seeds are only a few healthier fats that may aid in weight loss. However, bear in mind that healthy fat has a high-calorie content, so restrict your consumption. Instead of consuming fat overall, consider substituting these suitable fat types for your diet's bad fats.

6. Drink Healthier Beverages

One of the most straightforward approaches to improve fat burning is to replace sugar-sweetened beverages with nutritious alternatives.

Sugar-sweetened foods, such as soda and juice, are high in calories and have no health benefits. Alcohol is rich in calories and lowers inhibitions, causing you to be more prone to overeating. Sugar-sweetened drinks and alcohol intake have also been related to an elevated incidence of belly fat in research.

Limiting the consumption of these drinks will help you cut calories and sustain a healthier weight. Choose calorie-free drinks like water or green tea instead. Drinking (500 ml) of water before foods improved weight reduction by 4.4 pounds (2 kg) relative to a placebo group in a 12-week trial.

Green tea is another excellent option. It includes caffeine and is high in antioxidants, all of which can aid in fat burning and a metabolism enhancement.

Green tea extract, for example, improved fat burning by 12% as opposed to a placebo in a 12-adult trial. It's simple to encourage fat burning by substituting a bottle of water or a cup of green tea with one or two portions of high-calorie drinks.

7. Fill up on Fiber

Soluble fiber retains water and travels steadily across the digestive tract, enabling you to feel fuller over more extended periods.

According to some studies, increasing your consumption of high-fiber foods can protect you from weight gain and fat accumulation. Also, without incorporating any other nutritional or workout adjustments, participants in one survey of 1,114 adults shed 3.7% of their belly fat over five years with every 10-gram rise in soluble fiber consumption each day.

Another study discovered that increasing fiber intake made people feel fuller and helped them eat less. A regular rise of 14 grams of fiber was related to a 10% reduction in calorie intake. Not just that, but it was also attributed to a four-month weight reduction of almost 4.4 pounds (2 kg). High-fiber foods contain fruits, berries, legumes, whole grains, nuts, and seeds, to name a couple. They will help you burn fat and lose weight.

8. Cut Down on Refined Carbs

Reducing your intake of processed carbohydrates can aid in weight loss.

Refined grains are deprived of their bran and germ during fermentation, resulting in a low-fiber, low-nutrient finished product. Refined carbohydrates can have a higher glycemic index and may trigger blood sugar surges and crashes, leading to intensified appetite.

A high-refined-carbohydrate diet has been linked to a rise in belly fat in studies. A diet rich in whole grains, on the other hand, has been linked to a lower BMI and body weight, as well as a smaller waist circumference.

An analysis of 2,834 people found that those who consumed more processed grains had more disease-promoting belly fat, and those who ate primarily whole grains had less. Reduce refined carbohydrates' consumption from pastries, dried meats, pasta, white pieces of bread, and breakfast cereals for better outcomes. Whole grains like quinoa, whole wheat, buckwheat, rye, and oats may be substituted.

9. Increase Your Cardio

Cardio, also defined as cardiovascular exercise, is a form of exercise that targets the heart and lungs. Using exercise in your workout may be one of the most potent ways to improve weight loss.

One study of 16 experiments showed that the more physical workout people performed, the less abdominal fat they acquired. Aerobic activity has been shown in other research to raise muscle mass while decreasing abdominal fat, waist circumference, and body fat.

Most studies prescribe 150–300 minutes of mild to intensive exercise each week or 20–40 minutes of cardio per day. Running, jumping, cycling, and swimming are only a couple of the aerobic workouts that will help you shed weight and burn fat.

10.   Drink Coffee

Caffeine is a central component in virtually any fat-burning supplement and for a good cause. Coffee contains caffeine, which stimulates the central nervous system, increases appetite, and aids in the breakdown of fatty acids. Caffeine use has been shown in experiments to temporarily raise energy intake and boost metabolism by 3–11%.

Over 12 years, a significant study affecting over 58,000 participants showed that increased caffeine consumption was related to less weight gain. Another survey of 2,623 participants showed that higher caffeine consumption was related to a higher weight loss maintenance rate. Miss the milk and sugar in your coffee to get the most nutritional benefits. Instead, drink it black or with a tiny quantity of milk to avoid piling on the calories.

11. Try High-Intensity Interval Training (HIIT)

HIIT, or high-intensity interval training, is a form of exercise that involves rapid bursts of movement followed by short rest times to maintain an elevated heart rate.

HIIT has been shown in studies to be highly successful at increasing fat burning and encouraging weight loss. Young men who performed HIIT for twenty minutes, three times weekly, shed an average of (2 kg) of body fat over 12 weeks, despite making no other dietary or behavioral improvements, according to one report.

They also had a 17% drop in body fat and a substantial decline in waist circumference. In comparison to other types of cardio, HIIT can help you burn more calories in less time.

According to one report, HIIT helped people eat up to 30% more calories in the same period than other exercise forms like walking or jogging. Try switching between jogging, walking, or sprinting for 30 seconds at a time to get acquainted with HIIT.

12. Add Probiotics to Your Diet

Probiotics are healthy microbes that live in the digestive tract, which have been proven to improve various health outcomes. Research has shown that the bacteria in your gut plays a role in anything from immunity to mental wellbeing.

Whether by diet or supplementation, increasing probiotic consumption can also aid in fat burning and weight management.

People who took probiotics had slightly lower body weight, fat level, and body mass index than people who took a placebo, according to a study of 15 reports. Another research found that consuming probiotic supplements prevented fat and weight gain in people who ate a high-fat, high-calorie diet.

Certain Lactobacillus probiotic strains may be particularly effective in assisting weight and fat loss. Taking supplements is a convenient and fast way to get a daily dose of probiotics. Alternatively, probiotic-rich items such as kefir, natto, tempeh, kombucha, kimchi, and sauerkraut may be added to the diet.

13. Increase Your Iron Intake

Iron is a vital mineral that has a variety of roles in the body. Iron deficiency—like other nutrients like iodine—can influence the health of your thyroid gland. This tiny gland in your stomach secretes hormones that control your metabolism.

Low amounts of iron in the body have been related to reduced thyroid function and thyroid hormone development disruption in some studies.

Weakness, nausea, shortness of breath, and weight gain are common signs of hypothyroidism or reduced thyroid activity. Similarly, an iron deficiency may induce nausea, dizziness, headaches, and shortness of breath.

Treatment for iron deficiency will make your metabolism run more smoothly and battle exhaustion, allowing you to improve your activity level.

One research discovered that while 21 people were screened for iron deficiency, their body weight, waist circumference, and BMI all reduced. Unfortunately, many people's diets are deficient in iron. Iron deficiency is more common in women, babies, children, vegans, and vegetarians. To satisfy your iron requirements and boost your metabolism and energy levels, provide lots of iron-rich foods in your diet. Meat, fortified grains, fish cereals, dried fruits, leafy green vegetables, and beans all contain iron.

14. Give Intermittent Fasting a Shot

Intermittent fasting is a diet plan that alternates between feeding and fasting times. Intermittent fasting has been shown in experiments to aid weight reduction and fat loss. One study looked at the consequences of extended fasting, like alternate day fasting, which includes fasting and regularly eating on alternate days.

When paired with strength exercise, another small study found that feeding only over an eight-hour window per day helped reduce fat mass and preserve muscle mass. Intermittent fasting may take several forms, with some requiring you to eat only on some days of the week and some requiring you to eat only during reasonable times of the day.

Chapter 7: Hormonal Health of Women - The Most Ignored Factor in Weight Loss

Do you feel bloated, grumpy, or just not yourself? A hormonal disorder is likely to blame. Hormones are chemical "messengers" that affect the activity of your cells and organs. It's natural for your hormone levels to fluctuate during your life, such as before and after your cycle, throughout pregnancy, and menopause. However, certain drugs and health conditions may trigger them to fluctuate.

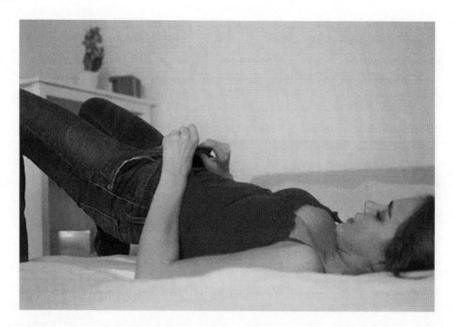

The average woman's cycle lasts 21 to 35 days. If yours doesn't come at the same period every month, even if you miss a few, it might suggest you're deficient in those hormones (estrogen and progesterone). Perimenopause, or the period of time before menopause, could occur whether you're in your 40s or early 50s. However, irregular intervals may be a sign of other health issues, such as polycystic ovarian syndrome (PCOS). Consult the surgeon.

Your hormones might be at work if you aren't having enough sleep or if the sleep you are getting isn't healthy. Progesterone, a hormone formed by the ovaries, assists in sleep. It may be difficult to fall and remain asleep if your levels are lower than average. Low estrogen levels can trigger hot flashes and night sweats, making it difficult to get the rest you need.

It's common to have a breakout before or after your cycle. On the other hand, acne that won't go away may be a sign of hormonal issues. Overworked oil glands may be caused by an imbalance of androgens (male hormones found in males and women). The skin cells in and near the hair follicles are often affected by androgens. Both items will worsen acne by clogging your pores.

Hormones have an unknown effect on the brain, according to experts. Changes in estrogen and progesterone will make the brain feel "foggy" and make it tough to recall things they realize. Some scientists believe estrogen affects neurotransmitters, which are chemicals found in the brain. During perimenopause and menopause, concentration and memory issues are persistent. They may, however, be a sign of other hormone-related issues, such as thyroid disorder. If you're having difficulty thinking straight, tell the doctor.

Receptors, tiny cells that react to estrogen and progesterone, line the inside of your stomach. You might find differences in how you digest food, whether certain hormones are higher or lower than average. That's why, before and throughout your time, diarrhea, bloating, stomach pain, and nausea can appear or worsen. Your hormone levels can be out of control at times if you're experiencing digestion problems as well as acne and exhaustion.

Are you constantly exhausted? One of the most prominent signs of a hormone deficiency is fatigue. Progesterone in abundance will render you sleepy. It will also drain your vitality if your thyroid—the butterfly-shaped gland in your stomach—produces minimal thyroid hormone. If your thyroid levels are too poor, an essential blood examination called a thyroid panel would inform you. You will be treated for that if they are.

According to researchers, drops in hormone levels or rapid shifts in their levels may trigger moodiness and the blues. Estrogen has an impact on serotonin, dopamine, and norepinephrine, which are essential brain chemicals. Other hormones, which obey the exact mechanisms as neurotransmitters, often affect how you feel.

You will want to eat more if you're feeling depressed or annoyed, as you may be when your estrogen levels decrease. Drops in the hormone have been related to weight gain, which may clarify why. Your body's leptin levels, a hormone that helps control food consumption, can also be influenced by the estrogen decrease.

A variety of factors may trigger these. Drops in estrogen, on the other hand, may cause menopause in certain people. That's why headaches are more likely right before or after your cycle when estrogen levels are down. Regular headaches, particularly those that occur about the same period per month, indicate that your levels of this hormone are fluctuating.

It's natural to experience this on occasion. However, if you're always dry or uncomfortable in your lower abdomen, low estrogen may be the cause. The hormone aids in keeping the vaginal tissue moist and relaxing. If the estrogen levels decrease due to a hormonal imbalance, it may induce vaginal dryness and tightness.

Your breast tissue can become less dense when your estrogen levels decrease. And a spike in the hormone may cause this tissue to thicken, perhaps resulting in new lumps or cysts. And if you don't have any other signs, speak to the doctor if you find any differences in your breasts.

7.1 Food and Female Hormones Are Connected

Hormones mean that we eat the necessary amount of food to sustain our bodies per day. They oversee informing the brain when it is time to feed and when it is time to avoid feeding. Obesity may be promoted if these signs do not work correctly.

Ghrelin is known as the "hunger hormone" because it signals to our brain that we are starving. It is created by the stomach, which stimulates appetite, food conversion to energy, and fat storage.

When we feed, fat cells produce leptin, which tells the brain that we're full.

7.2 How Your Diet Affects Your Hormones?

Hormones are the molecular messengers in the body. They play a role in almost every physiological mechanism, including metabolism, immunity, menstruation, and reproduction.

The proper functioning of the body needs a specific hormonal equilibrium. Certain items in your diet will either restore or throw off your hormone balance. It's essential to eat a well-balanced diet, particularly if you're going through menopause. Hormonal imbalances may trigger unpleasant symptoms during this transitional time of a woman's life. Learn how your food after menopause impacts your hormones.

1. Estrogen

The primary female sex hormone is estrogen. Estrogen is a hormone that controls the menstrual cycle and helps the uterus brace for birth. Your estrogen levels can fluctuate widely during perimenopause, the period preceding menopause. Your hormone levels decrease as you hit menopause. The effects of menopause are caused by hormone levels' fluctuations and the resulting decrease in estrogen levels. Hot flashes, mood fluctuations, night sweats, and menstrual irregularity are some of the signs. Estrogen cannot be obtained by food. Phytoestrogens, on the other hand, are used in a variety of plant foods. There are chemical classes that have a weak estrogenic effect on the body.

2. Insulin and Glucagon

Insulin is among the most well-known hormones that are controlled by what you consume. When you consume carbs, the glucose they provide enters your bloodstream. Your pancreas is triggered to produce insulin because of this. Insulin binds to glucose molecules and transports them to the cells, where they are converted to energy.

Another pancreatic enzyme is glucagon. Insulin has the same impact on it. Your pancreas produces glucagon while you go without food for a prolonged amount of time. This instructs the liver to transform glycogen accumulated in your body into glucose. The sugar is then secreted into the stomach, where it acts as an energy supply before you eat again. This physiological feedback mechanism is intended to maintain a constant blood sugar level.

Your pancreas generates insulin naturally, but your muscles, fat cells, and liver cells, do not react to it appropriately if you have insulin resistance. To support glucose, migrate through your tissues, your pancreas releases more insulin to compensate. Surplus blood sugar piles up in your body if your pancreas is unable to contain sufficient insulin. Insulin tolerance may progress to prediabetes or diabetes over time.

Your body transforms from gynoid, pear-shaped, or apple-shaped, when you approach menopause. According to some doctors, accumulating belly fat increases the chance of insulin resistance and diabetes.

3. Cortisol

The adrenal glands produce cortisol, which is also recognized as a stress hormone. It's a part of the body's fight-or-flight reflex, a hormonal response activated when you're stressed or in threat. Cortisol is essential to your life as part of your fight-or-flight reaction. Chronically elevated amounts of cortisol in the body, on the other hand, may boost blood pressure, stress levels, and visceral fat. This is the fat that envelops the midsection and gives it an apple appearance. Cortisol levels are particularly bothersome during menopause, since menopause already induces a change in body fat composition.

7.3 The Importance of a Well-Balanced Diet

Eating a well-balanced diet is vital for good health at every age. Avoid consuming more calories than you expend, since this can result in weight gain. Consume a wide range of vegetables, whole-grain foods, fruits, low-fat dairy products, and lean protein sources. Limit refined sugar, saturated and Trans-fats, and salt in "junk foods" that are poor in nutrients and heavy in calories. If you're going through menopause, soy or flaxseed products can help manage your symptoms and reduce your risk of developing health problems. It's also necessary to keep your caffeine and alcohol intake in check. Making a few changes to your dietary patterns will have a significant impact on your wellbeing.

7.4 Ten Natural Ways to Balance Your Hormones

Hormones play a significant role in mental, physical, and emotional well-being. These chemical messengers play a crucial role in appetite, weight, and mood regulation, among other items. Your endocrine glands usually generate the exact sum of each hormone necessary by different bodily processes.

On the other hand, hormonal imbalances have become more prevalent because of today's fast-paced urban lifestyle. Furthermore, when people mature, some hormones decline, and certain people suffer a more drastic decline than others. Fortunately, a well-balanced diet and other good lifestyle decisions will help you boost your hormone wellbeing and sound and work better.

1. Eat Enough Protein at Every Meal

It is essential to eat enough protein.

Dietary protein contains essential amino acids that your body cannot produce on its own and must be ingested daily to keep muscle, bone, and skin healthy. Protein also affects the release of hormones that regulate appetite and food consumption. According to research, protein consumption lowers ghrelin levels while increasing the output of hormones that make you feel whole, such as PYY and GLP-1.

According to one report, men developed 21% more GLP-1 and 13% more PYY after consuming a high-protein food rather than after eating a meal with a regular amount of protein. Furthermore, after the high-protein meal, participants' hunger levels dropped by 25% more than after the normal-protein meal.

Experts suggest eating an average of 20–30g of protein per meal to enhance hormone health. Having a portion of these high-protein foods with each meal is a simple way to do this.

2. Engage in Regular Exercise

Physical exercise has an essential effect on hormone wellbeing. Exercise has the potential to lower insulin levels and improve insulin sensitivity, which is a significant advantage.

Insulin is a hormone that has a variety of purposes. Allowing cells to absorb glucose and amino acids from the bloodstream, which are then used during energy and muscle maintenance, is one example.

Inflammation, diabetes, heart disease, and cancer have also been attributed to high insulin levels. They're often linked to insulin resistance, a disease in which your cells don't react appropriately to insulin signals.

Aerobic fitness, weight conditioning, and endurance exercise are also examples of physical activity that have been proven to boost insulin response and lower insulin levels.

Exercise improved insulin sensitivity and amounts of adiponectin, a hormone that has anti-inflammatory properties and helps control metabolism, in obese women throughout a 24-week trial.

Physical activity can also increase muscle-maintaining hormones, including testosterone, IGF-1, DHEA, and growth hormone, which decrease with age.

Even frequent walking can raise these hormone levels in people who cannot engage in vigorous exercise, significantly increasing strength and quality of life. While a mixture of resistance and aerobic exercise tends to yield the most significant outcomes, daily physical activity of any sort is helpful.

3. Avoid Sugar and Refined Carbs

Sugar and processed carbohydrates have been connected to a host of illnesses. Indeed, eliminating or reducing these foods can help hormone regulation and the prevention of obesity, diabetes, and other diseases.

Fructose has been shown in numerous studies to raise insulin levels and encourage insulin resistance, particularly in overweight and obese people who have pre-diabetes or diabetes. Fructose takes up about half of most sugars, which is essential. Honey and maple syrup are representations of natural sweets and high-fructose corn syrup and processed table sugar.

In one research, people with pre-diabetes who ate (50 grams) of honey, sugar, or high-fructose corn syrup observed similar insulin levels and insulin tolerance changes. Furthermore, a high-refined-carbohydrate diet, such as white bread and pretzels, can encourage insulin resistance in many adults and adolescents.

4. Learn to Manage Stress

Cortisol and adrenaline, commonly known as epinephrine, are two primary hormones that are caused by stress.

Since it lets the body deal with stress over time, cortisol is classified as "the stress hormone."

Adrenaline is the "fight-or-flight" hormone that gives the body a burst of adrenaline to help you respond quickly to danger.

Except for hundreds of years ago, when these hormones were primarily activated by predatory attacks, they are now primarily triggered by people's hectic, sometimes exhausting lifestyles.

Unfortunately, constant tension keeps cortisol levels up, which may contribute to overeating and obesity, as well as a rise in belly fat.

High blood pressure, a fast heart rhythm, and fear are also symptoms of elevated adrenaline levels. Adrenaline, unlike cortisol, is not prone to become excessively high because these effects are generally short-lived.

According to studies, stress-reduction approaches such as meditation, yoga, massage, and listening to calming music, will help you reduce your cortisol levels.

Massage therapy not only decreased cortisol levels by 31% on average but also boosted concentrations of the mood-boosting hormone serotonin by 29% and dopamine by 30% on average, according to a 2005 analysis of research.

And if you don't think you have the opportunity, strive to commit at least 10–15 minutes a day to stress-relieving practices.

5. Consume Healthy Fats

Incorporating high-quality natural fats into your diet can aid in the reduction of insulin resistance and hunger.

MCTs (medium-chain triglycerides) are a form of fat picked up by the liver and used as the energy right away.

They've been seen to support those who are overweight or obese and those who have diabetes, minimizing insulin resistance.

Coconut oil, palm oil, and pure MCT oil also contain MCTs.

Furthermore, studies show that eating healthy fat at meals causes the release of hormones like GLP-1, PYY, and cholecystokinin, which make you feel complete and happy (CCK).

Trans-fats, on the other hand, have been shown to enhance insulin tolerance and belly fat storage.

Consume a balanced fat source at each meal to boost hormone health.

6. Avoid Overeating and Undereating

Eating too much or too little will induce hormone adjustments, which can contribute to weight gain.

Overeating has been shown to raise insulin levels and decrease insulin sensitivity, mainly in insulin-resistant overweight and obese people.

According to one report, insulin-resistant obese individuals who consumed a 1,300-calorie meal had about twice as much insulin as thin people and "metabolically healthy" obese people who ate the same meal.

On the other hand, significantly lowering the calorie intake will boost the stress hormone cortisol levels, which has been related to weight gain when levels are significant.

According to one report, limiting food consumption to fewer than 1,200 calories a day caused cortisol levels to rise.

Interestingly, a 1996 study indicates that highly low-calorie diets could stimulate insulin resistance in certain people, which you would expect to find in people with diabetes.

Maintaining hormone equilibrium and a good weight may be achieved by eating around your calorie range.

7. Drink Green Tea

Green tea is one of the best healthy drinks on the market.

It produces an antioxidant known as epigallocatechin gallate (EGCG), which has been linked to a variety of health benefits, in addition to the metabolism-boosting caffeine.

According to research, green tea use has been shown to improve insulin sensitivity and lower insulin levels in both healthier people and those with insulin-resistant diseases like obesity and diabetes.

A few regulated trials showed that green tea did not appear to reduce insulin resistance or insulin levels when opposed to a placebo. Specific reactions, though, may have affected the findings.

You may want to consume one to three cups of green tea a day because it has other health benefits, and several reports say it will help with insulin reaction.

8. Eat Fatty Fish Often

Long-chain omega-3 fatty acids, which have potent anti-inflammatory effects, are present in abundance in fatty fish.

They can also benefit hormonal wellbeing, according to studies, by decreasing concentrations of the stress hormones cortisol and adrenaline.

Small research investigated how omega-3 fats affected men's results on an emotional stress scale.

The research discovered that when men ate a diet high in omega-3 fats for three weeks, their cortisol and epinephrine levels during the research were slightly lower than when they ate their regular diet.

Furthermore, rising the consumption of long-chain omega-3 fatty acids has been shown in several trials to minimize insulin resistance connected to obesity, polycystic ovary syndrome, and gestational diabetes.

Gestational diabetes develops in people who have never had diabetes since becoming pregnant. Insulin tolerance and high blood sugar levels describe it, much the same as type 2 diabetes.

Women with gestational diabetes were given 1,000 mg of omega-3 fatty acids lasting six weeks in one trial.

9. Get Consistent, High-Quality Sleep

No matter how good your food is or how much workout you receive, your health will suffer if you don't get enough restorative sleep.

Many hormones, including insulin, leptin, cortisol, ghrelin, and growth hormone, have been related to inadequate sleep.

Insulin sensitivity was reduced by 20% on average in one sample of men whose sleep was limited to five hours a night for one week.

Another research investigated how sleep deprivation affected stable young men.

When they were deprived of sleep for two days, their leptin levels fell by 18%, their ghrelin levels grew by 28%, and their hunger levels rose by 24%. Furthermore, the men wanted to consume high-calorie, high-carbohydrate diets.

Furthermore, it is not just the amount of sleep you receive that counts. The quality of your sleep is often crucial.

Your brain needs continuous sleep to complete all five phases of the sleep cycle. This is particularly essential for growth hormone production, which happens mostly at night throughout deep sleep.

10.   Consume a High-Fiber Diet

Fiber, especially soluble fiber, is an essential part of a balanced diet.

According to studies, it enhances insulin sensitivity and activates the release of hormones that make you feel complete and happy.

Although soluble fiber has the most impact on hunger and eating, insoluble fiber can also impact.

In one analysis of overweight and obese people, eating oligofructose, a form of soluble fiber, increased PYY levels, whereas cellulose, an insoluble fiber, appeared to increase GLP-1 levels.

Both forms of fiber helped people feel fuller for longer.

Make sure you consume fiber-rich meals regularly to prevent insulin tolerance and overeating.

Chapter 8: Intermittent Fasting: The Ideal Way of Life for Women Over 50

8.1 The Practice of Intermittent Fasting

Intermittent fasting may be achieved in several ways, though many people choose various types. Continue reading to learn about seven different ways to fast intermittently.

1. **Fast for 12 hours a day**

The diet's guidelines are straightforward. Every day, a person must select and observe a 12-hour fasting frame.

Fasting for 11–16 hours allows the body to transform fat reserves into energy, releasing ketones into the bloodstream. This should help you drop weight.

For beginners, this form of intermittent fasting strategy may be a reasonable alternative. This is because the fasting window is comparatively short, much of the fasting happens while sleeping, and the individual will eat the same number of calories per day.

The most convenient approach to complete the 12-hour fast is to have sleep time in the fasting window.

An individual might, for example, fast between the hours of 7 p.m. and 7 a.m. They'd have to end dinner at 7 p.m. and fast before 7 a.m. to eat breakfast, but they'd be sleeping for most of the period in between.

2. Fasting for 16 hours

The 16:8 cycle, also known as the Leangains diet, involves fasting for 16 hours a day and only feeding for 8 hours.

Men fast for 16 hours a day, and women fast for 14 hours on the 16:8 diet. This intermittent fasting method could be beneficial for those who have attempted the 12-hour fast and found it to be ineffective.

People who fast this way typically finish their evening meal by 8 p.m., miss breakfast the next day, and don't eat again before noon.

Even though mice consumed the same overall number of calories as mice that ate anytime they wanted, a report on mice showed that reducing the feeding window to 8 hours saved them from obesity, diabetes, inflammation, and liver disease.

3. Fasting for two days a week

The 5:2 diet allows individuals to consume an average amount of nutritious food for five days and then decrease their calorie consumption for the next two days.

Men usually eat 600 calories and women 500 calories over the two fasting days.

Fasting days are usually separated during the week. They can, for example, fast on Mondays and Thursdays and eat normally for the rest of the week. Between fasting days, there should be at least one non-fasting day.

The 5:2 diet, also recognized as the Fast diet, has received little research. A sample of 107 overweight or obese people discovered that calorie restriction twice weekly and constant calorie restriction also resulted in similar weight loss.

The diet also decreased insulin levels and increased insulin sensitivity in the patients, according to the report.

The results of this fasting type on 23 overweight women were studied in a small-scale analysis. The women lost 4.7 % of their body weight and 8.0 % of their excess body fat in one menstrual period. After 5 days of the regular diet, the bulk of the women's measurements returned to normal.

4. Alternate day fasting

The alternate-day fast plan, which includes fasting every other day, has many variants.

Some people observe alternate day fasting by refusing solid foods on fasting days, while others accommodate up to 500 calories. People always want to consume as much as they want on feeding days.

According to one research, alternate fasting is successful for weight loss and cardiac well-being in both lean and overweight people. Throughout a 12-week cycle, the 32 participants lost a total of 5.1 (kg), or just over 11 (lb.).

Alternate-day fasting is a more severe type of intermittent fasting that may not be appropriate for beginners or people with such medical conditions. This method of fasting can even be challenging to sustain over time.

5. A weekly 24-hour fast

In a 24-hour diet, teas and calorie-free beverages are permissible.

The Eat-Stop-Eat diet means living without eating for 24 hours for one to two days a week. Some people fast from one meal to the next.

People on this diet plan will drink wine, tea, and other calorie-free beverages during the fasting time.

On non-fasting days, people should resume their daily eating habits. This form of eating decreases a person's overall calorie consumption, thus keeping the individual's food preferences unregulated.

Fasting for 24 hours can be challenging, leading to nausea, headaches, and irritability. As the body responds to this new eating routine, many people feel that these symptoms become less severe with time.

Before attempting the 24-hour fast, people can benefit from attempting a 12-hour or 16-hour fast.

6. Meal skipping

Beginners can benefit from this versatile approach to intermittent fasting. It entails missing meals on occasion.

People may choose which meals to miss based on their hunger levels or time constraints. It is, however, essential to consume healthy foods at each meal.

Individuals who track and react to their bodies' hunger signals are more prone to succeed at meal skipping. People who practice intermittent fasting feed when they are hungry and miss meals when they are not.

For certain people, this may sound more normal than the other fasting approaches.

7. The Warrior Diet

The Warrior Diet is a form of intermittent fasting that is very severe.

During a 20-hour fasting time, the Warrior Diet entails consuming very little, usually only a few portions of raw fruit and vegetables, and only enjoying one full meal at night. In most cases, the feeding time is just 4 hours long.

This intermittent fasting method could be better for people who have already experienced other intermittent fasting methods.

The Warrior Diet advocates argue that humans are nocturnal eaters and that feeding at night helps the body gain nutrients according to its circadian rhythms.

People can make sure to eat lots of greens, meats, and healthy fats over the 4-hour feeding period. Carbohydrates can also be used.

Although it is possible to consume certain items during fasting time, adhering to the rigid rules for what and when to eat in the long run can be difficult. Furthermore, some people find it daunting to consume such a big meal too close to bedtime.

There's even a possibility that people on this diet won't receive enough nutrients like fiber. This will raise cancer incidence and have a detrimental influence on digestive and immune function.

8.2 Tips for Maintaining Intermittent Fasting

Intermittent fasting can be rendered possible with meditation and moderate workouts. The following suggestions will help people stay on board and get the most out of intermittent fasting:

- Keeping yourself hydrated: Throughout the day, consume plenty of water and calorie-free beverages like herbal teas.

- Refraining from obsessing about food: On fasting days, plan many distractions to keep you from worrying about food, such as catching up on paperwork or seeing a movie.

- Sleeping and relaxing: On fasting days, avoid strenuous exercises, while light exercises such as yoga can be helpful.

- Counting every calorie: Choose nutrient-dense meals high in protein, fiber, and healthy fats if the preferred schedule requires any calories during fasting times. Corn, lentils, poultry, pork, almonds, and avocado are only a few examples.

- Eating a lot of calories: Choose foods that are both filling and low in calories, such as popcorn, fresh veggies, and fruits with strong water content, such as grapes and melon.

- Rising flavor without consuming calories: Garlic, herbs, sauces, or vinegar may be used liberally to season meals. These foods are deficient in calories but high in taste, helping to alleviate hunger pangs.

- During the fasting time, choose nutrient-dense foods: Consuming diets rich in fiber, minerals, vitamins, and other nutrients helps maintain blood sugar levels to avoid nutritional deficiencies. A well-balanced diet will help you lose weight and improve your general health.

8.3 Intermittent Fasting 30 Days Challenge

Intermittent fasting has been shown to boost fitness, retard aging, and aid in weight loss or maintenance. So, let's do it for 30 days to see if we can't transform it into a permanent routine. There are now successful methods to do this. The following are the most critical considerations:

The first consideration is the time limit. The 12:12 method is the most straightforward. For people with chronic health problems like type 2 diabetes, research has found that a window of up to 16 hours may be beneficial. On the other hand, a longer fasting window can trigger you to become too hungry and overeat when you do feed, which is counterintuitive. As a result, we suggest beginning at 12:12 and steadily rising by 30-minute intervals before you reach the point that you feel "hungry" and stopping before that happens.

The second point to consider is hydration. Ensure you're well hydrated. When you first wake up, drink two whole glasses of water with nothing in it. This will not only offer you stamina and prevent you from misinterpreting dehydration for hunger, but it will also make you feel whole, which will help you avoid hunger for longer.

The third group is "cheating." Yeah, there is a trick to this that will cause you to have a longer, fasting window without feeling hungry. The trick to avoiding triggering your mTOR metabolic pathway while fasting is to stop it. To keep a long story short, protein and carbohydrates do this, but fat does not. However, no one needs 300 calories of fat in the morning. So, in your coffee, apply a splash of organic whole milk. This usually encourages me to get to a 14-hour window without looking like I'm going to consume my couch.

Chapter 9: Intermittent Fasting and Exercise

When it comes to cultivating longevity, both intermittent fasting (IF) and exercise are essential, but should you combine the two? Let's go through what you need to know about exercising when fasting.

Is It Necessary to Work Out When Fasting?

Yes, you should work out while fasting and hormone optimization, not just calories and exercise, is the secret to weight loss and muscle gain. Intermittent fasting has been seen to have impressive effects of its own, but mixing it with sprint training raises the benefits of both to an entirely new degree. When you mix the two, you'll get more growth hormones and be more insulin-responsive, which is essential for remaining young and lean. Many people worry about calories in vs. calories out and are worried about muscle loss, which will arise if you work out without refueling.

Can We Exercise On An Empty Stomach?

Exercising on an empty stomach is not only appropriate, but it also enhances the advantages of both exercise and fasting. This is a multi-therapeutic strategy, in which the synergy between two health-promoting items enhances each other's advantages to the degree that exceeds the number of their benefits. Working out in the morning before eating is one of the easiest ways to enjoy these rewards.

Intermittent Fasting and Working Out

Running out before breakfast is yet another way of suggesting you work out when on an irregular fast. An intermittent fast is anytime the body goes without food for a period of time (including while you're sleeping) over 24 hours. The period of your sporadic fast should be between 16 and 18 hours to enjoy the maximum benefits. Eat between both the hours of 10:30 a.m. and 6:30 p.m., for example.

When to Work Out While Intermittent Fasting?

To support the body's normal circadian cycle, the safest time to exercise during intermittent fasting usually is right after waking up or shortly after. Working out (or eating) too near to bedtime has been seen to disrupt deep and REM sleep stages, so save the workout for the next day.

You shouldn't eat right after exercise for the same reasons you shouldn't eat right after a fasted run: hormone optimization. According to studies, waiting two to three hours after exercise before eating stimulates an increase in growth hormone, which aids in fat burning and energy replacement (sugar). A hormone change happens because of adaptation to the discomfort induced by a high-intensity exercise. If your routine just provides for a lunchtime workout, you will exercise at that time and then enjoy the hormone effects from not consuming for two or three hours afterward.

Cardio and Intermittent Fasting

The hormonal benefits of fasting-induced exercise are attributed to the loss of muscle and liver glycogen reserves that happens while you fast. It's OK to exercise during intermittent fasting, but the results will be determined by how fat-adapted the body is. You should anticipate a slight reduction in results if you're new to fasting and exercise; it can take up to six months for certain athletes to completely transition their strength to this new food source. If you're a competitive runner, for example, and your focus is to improve your race results, don't turn to fasted training a few weeks before a meet. If you're performing exercise when fasted, don't keep the fast going during the workout; instead, refuel afterward.

Sprint Training and Intermittent Fasting

Sprint exercise, also known as high-intensity interval training (HIIT), comprises 15–30-minute intervals of physical action accompanied by rest periods. Not only is sprint training time adequate, but studies show that it has health benefits that aerobic activity alone cannot offer, such as a substantial rise in human growth hormone (HGH). Sprint exercise has many advantages, including enhanced muscle and brainpower and endurance, increased growth hormone, improved body structure, improved brain activity, higher testosterone levels, and reduced depression. Many of these advantages are enhanced as sprint running is combined with intermittent fasting. Sprint training is an excellent way to add fitness into your fasted time, and you can extend your fast two to three hours afterward to reap further benefits.

Lifting Weights and Fasting

Lifting weights during fasting is also appropriate, but you should be aware of the role glucose performs in muscle repair after a considerable weight-lifting period, particularly while fasted. Your glycogen reserves are still exhausted as you work out when fasted. If your day's exercise requires hard lifting, you should do it when fasted, but you can eat a meal right afterward. Heavy lifting puts enough tension on the body to necessitate an urgent refeed. Lifting weights when fasted, like cardio, can reduce your intensity in the short term as your body adjusts to being a "fat burner." As a result, you may want to reserve your weight-lifting workouts for after you've eaten (in this case, you should fast for two to three hours afterward) and include fasted exercise on days where you do burst-style training.

9.1 Why May People Exercise While Fasting?

When exercising while fasting, one should take the requisite precautions. Exercise is permissible for people who are fasting. Some people work out while IF because they think it will improve their fitness. These are some of the reasons:

Loss in weight

When people consume carbohydrates, their bodies turn them into glucose, a kind of sugar. Glucose is stored in the body as glycogen.

According to a study, glycogen stocks are exhausted during fasting times. This indicates that the body has begun to burn fat. Weight reduction can be aided by this reliable source of energy during exercise.

According to one report, exercising when fasted resulted in more significant weight reduction than exercising during a meal.

People who fasted overnight and exercised did not lose more weight than someone who fed before exercising, according to a 2014 survey. Another mouse research found that whether combined with or without exercise, it resulted in successful weight reduction.

Autophagy

Autophagy is the act of consuming one's own body.

According to the results of studies on exercise and fasting, it can improve autophagy.

Autophagy is a cellular mechanism that aids in the destruction of unwanted or weakened cells to restore younger, healthier ones.

Anti-aging

According to a 2018 report, IF and exercise can slow down the aging and disease processes. This is attributed to the reality that IF and exercise will affect metabolism.

9.2 Why It Might Not Be Effective?

Exercise during fasting has also been related to several possibly harmful side effects, according to studies. This can involve things like:

- Reduced performance: Research indicates that IF can reduce exercise intensity, particularly in highly trained athletes.

- Struggle to muscle building: A 2018 randomized clinical study showed that IF males gained less muscle than someone who consumed regular meals. IF, on the other side, has no detrimental effects on their muscle retention. Another research backs this up, claiming that IF will help preserve muscle mass.

- Lightheadedness: Both IF and exercise will help to relieve blood pressure. An individual can feel lightheadedness because of mixing the two due to the drop in blood pressure.

- Blood Sugar Levels: If you combine IF with exercise, the blood sugar levels will decrease. If a person's sugar levels sink too low, they will pass out.

Fasting and fitness literature seems to have contradictory findings. IF for weight reduction can be helpful based on a person's fitness objectives. Alternative foods, on the other hand, may be used for those who choose to gain weight.

9.3 Planning the Workout

To keep healthy throughout IF, exercises should be planned over time. Here are few things to think about:

- Type of workout: Aerobic and anaerobic exercise are the two forms of exercise. Aerobic activity, also known as 'cardio,' is done for a long time, such as running, biking, or cycling. Anaerobic exercise is any practice that involves a high degree of intensity over a limited amount of time, such as weightlifting or sprinting. The type of fast an individual follows would most definitely determine the type of workout they perform. An individual doing 16:8 or nightly fasts, for example, may do aerobic or anaerobic exercise during their feeding hours. When anyone is performing alternating days and needs to work out on their non-eating days, they should generally adhere to a lower-intensity aerobic practice.

- Workout timing: While a person can exercise while fasting, it is always preferred to do so after a meal.

- Food type: If you're about to exercise and sleep, you can think about what you will consume. A lunch 2–3 hours before exercise, should be used in pre-workout nutrition. It can be substantial in complex carbohydrates and protein, such as whole-grain cereal.

9.4 Safety Tips

When you've planned the workout, keep the following protection measures in mind:

- Walking during fasting times: This would offer an individual the stamina they need to perform a workout. When exercising after eating, though, every form of exercise is typically healthy.

- Paying attention to what the body is telling you: When anyone happens to feel sick when exercising while on IF, they can quit instantly.

- Staying hydrated: It is essential to stay hydrated during a workout, even if you are not IF. Since water makes up most of the human body, it is essential to replenish fluids drained during exercise. If an individual has chronic health issues but wants to try IF and work out, they should talk to their doctor first.

Chapter 10: Understanding of Metabolism and Fasting

Surprisingly, evidence indicates intermittent fasting has the same or less harmful impacts on metabolism than regular dieting. Many people assume intermittent fasting increases metabolism because it results in less lean body mass loss and more of fat burning. While it's difficult to lose weight without sacrificing any lean body mass, evidence shows that intermittent fasting loses a smaller proportion of lean body mass than traditional dieting. The body's calorie-burning rate slows while lean body mass is preserved. On the other hand, short fasting times allow the body to enter fat reserves and burn a higher proportion of fat mass for energy.

Intermittent fasting (IF) is a form of eating that includes fasting cycles followed by regular eating. This eating pattern will help you lose weight, lower your risk of disease, and extend your life. Some researchers also argue that it is a better way to reduce weight than traditional calorie restriction because of the metabolic benefits.

10.1 Intermittent Fasting Is Extremely Effective for Loss of Weight

Intermittent fasting is a quick, efficient, and reasonably easy-to-follow fat-loss technique.

Intermittent fasting has been found in experiments to be almost as efficient as, if not more effective than, traditional calorie restriction when it comes to weight reduction.

According to a 2014 study, intermittent fasting can help people lose 3–8% of their body weight in only 3–24 weeks.

Furthermore, a new study suggested intermittent fasting could be a healthier weight-loss strategy for overweight and obese people than very-low-calorie diets.

Surprisingly, this form of eating can even be helpful to your metabolism and general health.

Intermittent fasting can be achieved in several forms. The 5:2 diet, which includes fasting two days a week, is followed by specific individuals. Others follow the 16/8 approach or alternate day fasting.

Intermittent fasting is a perfect way to reduce weight. It will even help you lose weight and increase your metabolic fitness.

10.2 Intermittent Fasting Rises Many Fat Burning Hormones

Hormones are chemical messengers that help us communicate with one another. They migrate around the body to help complex processes like development and metabolism run smoothly. They also play a significant role in weight management. This is attributed to the reality that they have a significant effect on your appetite, the number of calories you ingest, and the volume of fat you accumulate or burn.

Improvements in the balance of certain fat-burning hormones have been attributed to intermittent fasting. This might render it an efficient weight-loss tool.

Insulin

Insulin is a hormone that plays a crucial role in fat metabolism. It tells the body to accumulate fat and prevents it from being broken down. Having chronically elevated insulin levels will make losing weight even more challenging. Obesity, type 2 diabetes, cardiac disease, and cancer have also been related to elevated insulin levels. Intermittent fasting is almost as good at reducing insulin levels as calorie-restricted diets. This eating style has been shown to lower fasting insulin levels by 20–31%.

The Hormone of Human Growth

Fasting may increase human growth hormone levels in the blood, which is an essential hormone for fat loss. Fasting has been found to raise the amount of human growth hormone in men by up to fivefold in research. Increases in HGH levels in the blood stimulate fat burning while still preserving muscle mass and providing other benefits. On the other hand, women don't necessarily reap the same benefits from fasting as males, and it's unclear if women would see the same increase in human growth hormone.

Norepinephrine

Norepinephrine, a tension hormone that increases alertness and concentration aids the "fight or flight" reaction. It has a host of other impacts on the body, one of which is inducing fatty acid release in your fat cells. Increased norepinephrine levels usually result in more fat being accessible for the body to burn.

10.3 Advantages of Having Good Metabolism

Toxin removal from the body

Via bowel motions, perspiration, and urination, a balanced metabolism will help cleanse and eliminate the waste and pollutants that have developed in the body. Toxins harm a variety of bodily functions as well as the metabolic rate. Diuretic diets and detoxification can aid in the enhancement of the body's natural abilities.

Blood Circulation improvement

Blood not only transports carbohydrates and oxygen but also helps the intestines remove contaminants and waste. In other terms, a faster metabolism will help micronutrient absorption and transportation. They share direct benefits such as warm hands and feet, better nutrient absorption, and increased energy. Any individual could also be able to avoid edema by growing their water metabolism.

Boosting the mood

People with a fast appetite are more likely to be cheerful and help the nervous system work properly. As the metabolism slows, less nutrition is transported by the blood to nourish the autonomic nervous system, resulting in fear, boredom, frustration, and other depressing symptoms. Maintaining a healthy metabolism will lead to more energy and a more optimistic disposition.

Appearance of adolescents

Higher metabolic speeds will also help you shed weight and tighten your skin naturally, as well as improve your overall physical performance. The benefit goes to the joint efforts of enhanced blood supply, increased oxygen, and metabolized contaminants and wastes once again.

Increasing your natural immunity

As you already remember, white blood cells are the first line of protection for the immune system. They're contained in the blood, and we all know how important good blood circulation is for metabolism. Using metabolism boosters will help you battle age and illness by boosting your immunity.

More energy

A sluggish metabolic rate is caused by a poor diet and a lack of energy, making you feel exhausted and sleepy all the time. In an ideal world, the body will need a certain amount of energy to sustain simple breathing, standing, and other similar tasks at the necessary metabolic rate. If you don't have enough resources, you won't sustain the most important biochemical functions, which can slow down your weight loss.

Metabolism Boosting Tips

- Eat well.

- Exercise daily.

- Avoid eating late at night.

- Make sure you have enough water.

Metabolism Boosting Foods

- Maca

- Cayenne pepper

- Garcinia Cambogia

- Ginger

- Lemons

Healthy Snacks to Increase Metabolism

- Almonds

- Celery

- Berries

- Chia Seeds

Does Green Tea Boost Your Metabolism?

Green tea is one of the most powerful metabolism boosters. It is a natural stimulant that incorporates caffeine. It will help you eat calories and raise your heart rate, which will in turn help release fatty acids stored in your body to provide energy. Green tea intake as part of a regular routine has a range of possible health advantages, including cardiac health, suspected anti-aging effects, and the capacity to improve metabolism. It's loaded with antioxidants and can be used as a supplement or as a tea. Green tea also aids in L-theanine production, an amino acid that promotes alertness in the body.

10.4 Disadvantages of Having High or Low Metabolism

A person with a quick metabolism may fail to gain or retain weight for a prolonged period in certain instances. This is especially challenging for expectant mothers since weight gain is critical for both the baby and the mother's wellbeing. Through eating for two, a woman will have healthy nutrition and fuel for herself and the infant. Consequently, that is a drawback that a pregnant woman would continue to consult together with a doctor to ensure that she feeds enough for two to maintain a safe baby.

A fast metabolism has an immediate impact on blood sugar levels. Blood sugar levels begin to decrease during the day as the body turns carbohydrates into energy rapidly, resulting in rapid heartbeat, irritability, and heavy sweating. Maintaining a stable blood sugar level is essential for everyone, ensuring that anyone with a fast metabolism needs more time throughout the day to consume as much as possible.

High metabolism's health consequences may be mitigated by eating often. In certain circumstances, though, a doctor can prescribe a medication to slow down the rate of metabolism. This may quickly contribute to hyperthyroidism, a disorder marked by the release of various hormones that accelerate metabolism.

In certain situations, an elevated metabolic rate is related to a high mortality rate. In the end, this may easily contribute to several life-threatening problems. The other aspect that leads to high mortality is oxidative harm in people who have a rapid metabolism.

Many people believe that having a fast metabolism is a benefit, but the fact is that it comes with a lot of dangers. As a result, maintaining a stable metabolic rate is critical for leading a healthy lifestyle.

Chapter 11: Detox Your Body

Detox diets are usually short-term nutritional measures that seek to rid the body of contaminants. A traditional detox diet includes a fasting time supplemented by a strict diet of fruits, herbs, fruit juices, and liquids. Herbs, teas, vitamins, and colon cleanses, or enemas are also used in detox.

Improved circulation

Detox treatments are often prescribed because of possible sensitivity to harmful contaminants in the atmosphere or the diet. Pollutants, toxic substances, heavy metals, and other hazardous materials are among them. Obesity, digestion disorders, autoimmune diseases, nausea, allergies, bloating, and chronic exhaustion, are among the health complications these diets are said to cope with. There are several options to perform a detox diet—varying from complete hunger fasts to easier food changes.

At least one of the following is used with most detox diets:

- Fasting for one or three days.

- Drinking new fruit and vegetable drinks, smoothies, water, and tea.

- Just drinking such drinks, including salted water or lemon juice.

- Food rich in heavy metals, toxins, and allergens should be prevented.

- Take natural or nutritional supplements.

- Eliminating all allergenic ingredients for a period before eventually reintroducing them.

- Use laxatives, bowel cleanses, or enemas to alleviate constipation.

- Daily exercise; total abstinence from beer, caffeine, tobacco, and processed sugar.

11.1 How Does Detoxification Work?

Detoxification is the process of cleaning the blood. It is achieved by eliminating impurities from the liver's blood, which often processes contaminants for removal. During a body detox, toxins are also eliminated through the kidneys, lungs, intestines, lymphatic system, and skin. Impurities aren't fully filtered while processes are corrupted, and the body suffers as a result.

A body detox regimen will aid the body's natural healing mechanism by:

1. Fasting to rest the organs.

2. Activating the liver to force contaminants out of the body.

3. Promoting elimination from the intestines, kidneys, and skin.

4. Enhancing blood circulation.

5. Refueling the body with safe nutrients.

11.2 Ways of Detox Using Intermittent Fasting

Fasting has been a popular subject in the field of diet and for a good cause. According to a study, it's been related to several health effects, including weight reduction and lower blood sugar, triglyceride, cholesterol, insulin, and inflammatory levels. Furthermore, research suggests that fasting and calorie restriction, in general, can both slow down the aging process and improve cellular repair.

Fasting can also help boost the development and function of some detoxifying enzymes and the protection of your liver, one of the most important organs involved in the process. While fasting and calorie restriction can help you detox, your body has its mechanism for getting rid of waste and toxins.

1. Limit Alcohol

The liver is responsible for metabolizing more than 90% of all alcohol.

Alcohol is converted into acetaldehyde by liver enzymes and is a recognized cancer-causing chemical. Your liver recognizes acetaldehyde as a poison and transforms it into an innocuous product named acetate, then excreted. Although observational trials have found that low-to-moderate alcohol intake is good for cardiac health, heavy drinking can lead to many health issues.

Drinking too much alcohol will damage your liver by inducing fat accumulation, inflammation, and scarring. When this occurs, the liver cannot fulfill its vital roles, such as removing waste and other contaminants from the body. As a result, restricting or altogether avoiding alcohol is one of the most effective strategies to maintain the body's detoxification mechanism working smoothly.

According to health officials, alcohol consumption can be reduced to one drink a day for women and two beverages a day for men. If you don't drink now, you shouldn't start because of light-to-moderate alcohol's possible heart advantages. Drinking too much alcohol impairs the liver's capacity to perform basic tasks, including detoxification.

2. Focus on Sleep

To help your body's wellbeing and natural detoxification mechanism, you must get enough good sleep each night.

Sleeping helps the brain to reorganize and recharge while simultaneously eliminating hazardous waste byproducts that have accrued during the day.

A protein named beta-amyloid is one of these waste materials, and it plays a part in the development of Alzheimer's disease.

Since your body doesn't have enough time to execute specific tasks when you don't have enough sleep, contaminants will build up and adversely influence your health.

Stress, anxiety, elevated blood pressure, cardiac failure, type 2 diabetes, and obesity have also been attributed to poor sleep in the short and long term.

To preserve a healthy lifestyle, you should sleep seven to nine hours per night consistently.

If you're having difficulty staying or fall asleep at night, make behavioral adjustments, including keeping to a sleep routine and limiting blue light (emitted from smart devices and computer screens) before bed.

A good night's sleep helps the brain to reconfigure, recharge, and release pollutants that build up during the day.

3. Drink More Water

Water is fantastic for a lot more than just quenching thirst. It keeps the body calm, lubricates muscles, helps digestion and nutrient absorption, and detoxifies the body by reducing waste.

These operations, though, produce wastes in the form of urea and carbon dioxide, which may damage the body if they build up in your blood.

These waste materials are conveyed by water, easily removed by breathing, urination, or sweating. Consequently, remaining hydrated is essential for detoxification.

Water consumption should be (3.7 liters) for men and (2.7 liters) for women regularly. Depending on your lifestyle, where you live, and how active you are, you will need it.

4. Reduce Your Intake of Sugar and Processed Foods

Today's environmental health problems are believed to be caused by sugar and refined goods.

Obesity and other health disorders such as heart failure, cancer, and diabetes have been attributed to a heavy intake of sugary and heavily refined foods.

These diseases obstruct the body's standard detoxification mechanism by causing damage to vital organs such as your liver and kidneys.

High sugary soda intake, for example, may lead to fatty liver, a disorder that impairs liver function.

You will maintain the body's detoxification function by eating less fast food.

By leaving fast food on the supermarket shelf, you can restrict your intake. You're unlikely to be tempted if it's not in your kitchen.

It's also a good idea to replace fast food with nutritious options like fruits and vegetables to cut down on intake.

5. Eat Antioxidant-Rich Foods

Antioxidants shield the cells from free radicals, which inflict cell damage. Oxidative stress is a disorder that occurs when the body produces so many free radicals.

Your body typically generates these molecules for cellular processes, including digestion. However, excessive free radicals may be generated by alcohol, cigarette smoke, a poor diet, and pollution exposure.

These molecules have been linked to various disorders, including diabetes, heart failure, liver disease, asthma, and some forms of cancer, by inducing harm to the body's cells.

Excess free radicals and other contaminants induce oxidative stress, which raises the risk of cancer. Eating a diet high in antioxidants will help your body combat oxidative stress.

Concentrate on receiving antioxidants from your diet rather than supplements, which will also raise some diseases if consumed in significant quantities.

Vitamin A, vitamin C, selenium, vitamin E, lycopene, lutein, and zeaxanthin are all antioxidants.

Antioxidants are abundant in berries, bananas, seeds, caffeine, onions, herbs, and drinks such as coffee and green tea.

6. Eat Foods High in Prebiotics

A detoxification and excretion mechanism in the digestive cells safeguards the gut and body from harmful contaminants and chemicals.

Prebiotics, a kind of fiber that feeds the good bacteria in your gut known as probiotics, are the foundation of gut health. Your healthy bacteria will generate nutrients called short-chain fatty acids, which are suitable for your wellbeing, thanks to prebiotics.

Antibiotic use, poor oral care, and poor food quality may all cause the healthy bacteria in your gut to become unbalanced with the harmful bacteria.

As a result of this unfavorable change in microbiota, the immune and detoxification mechanisms can be weakened, increasing your likelihood of illness and inflammation.

Prebiotic-rich diets will help the immune and detoxification processes stay in good shape. Tomatoes, bananas, artichokes, asparagus, onions, garlic, and oats are good sources of prebiotics.

7. Decrease Your Salt Intake

Detoxing is a way for specific individuals to get rid of extra water.

If you have a disease that affects your kidneys or liver, or if you don't drink enough water, overeating salt will cause your body to absorb extra fluid.

Bloating and clothing discomfort may result from this excess fluid accumulation. If you consume a lot of salt, you should detox and get rid of the excess water weight.

Although it can seem counterintuitive, increasing the water intake is one of the most effective ways to lose extra water weight caused by excessive salt consumption.

When you overeat salt and drink too little water, the body produces an antidiuretic enzyme, which stops you from urinating and therefore detoxifying.

Your body decreases the antidiuretic hormone release and improves urination, allowing you to eliminate more fluids and waste material.

Raising the consumption of potassium-rich foods, which mitigate some of the effects of sodium, is also helpful. Potatoes, kidney beans, squash, bananas, and spinach, are also high in potassium.

8. Get Active

Regular activity is related to a healthy life and a decreased incidence of several illnesses and disorders, including type 2 diabetes, cardiac failure, elevated blood pressure, and some cancers, independent of body weight.

Although there are many factors at work regarding the health effects of exercise, one of the most important is decreased inflammation.

Although specific inflammation is essential for repairing wounds or recovering from illnesses, excessive inflammation weakens the body's processes and spreads disease.

Exercise will help the body's processes, as the detoxification mechanism works better and protects you from illness by reducing inflammation.

At least 150–300 minutes of moderate-intensity exercise a week, such as brisk walking, or 75–150 minutes of vigorous-intensity physical activity per week, such as running, is suggested.

11.3 Pros and Cons of Detox

Detox diets are widely used for rapid weight reduction, de-bloating, removing contaminants for improved fitness, among other marketed advantages. Detoxification services may last anywhere from three to seven days, or sometimes two weeks. Others require the usage of vitamins and other prepared items, whereas some merely include a limited list of foods to eat and a lengthy list of foods to avoid.

Although there are plenty of plans to pursue, there is a scarcity of high-quality research data to back up their use. If you're thinking of doing one of these diets, think of the benefits and drawbacks.

Pros

- May reset habits
- Quick weight loss
- Short-term benefits
- Limited-time effort

Cons

- Safety concerns
- Highly restrictive
- Reduced energy
- Lacking scientific support
- Can be expensive

Chapter 12: Intermittent Fasting Recipes

12.1 Grilled Lemon Salmon

Servings: 4 | Ready in 27 mins

Ingredients

- Fresh dill 2 teaspoons

- Pepper ½ teaspoon

- Salt ½ teaspoon

- Garlic powder ½ teaspoon

- Salmon fillet 1 ½ lbs.

- Brown sugar ¼ cup

- Chicken bouillon cube 1

- Water 3 tablespoons

- Soy sauce 3 tablespoons

- Oil 3 tablespoons

- Lemon 1

- Green onion 4 tablespoons

- Onions 2 slices

Directions

1. Sprinkle the salmon with dill, mustard, salt, and garlic powder.

2. Put it in a shallow glass pan.

3. Combine the sugar, chicken broth, fat, soy sauce, and green onions in a mixing bowl.

4. Pour the sauce over the salmon.

5. Cover and chill for 1 hr., flipping halfway through.

6. Drain and throw out the marinade.

7. Place onion and lemon on top of grill on medium fire.

8. Cook for 15 minutes, just until the fish is cooked through.

12.2 Shredded Brussels Sprouts along with Onions and Bacon

Servings: 6 | Ready in 30 mins

Ingredients

- Bacon 2 slices

- Yellow onion 1 small

- Salt ¼ teaspoon

- Water ¾ cup

- Dijon mustard 1 teaspoon

- Brussel sprouts 1 lb.

- Cedar vinegar 1 tablespoon

Directions

1. Cook bacon until crisp in a big skillet over medium heat (5–7 minutes); drain on paper towels, then scramble.

2. Place the onion and salt into the drippings in the pan and cook, constantly stirring, until tender and browned (around 3 minutes).

3. Scrape any browned bits with water and mustard, then add Brussels sprouts and fry, constantly stirring, until soft (4 to 6 minutes).

4. Add the vinegar and crumbled bacon on top.

12.3 Tilapia Parmesan

Servings: 4 | Ready in 35 mins

Ingredients

- Tilapia fillets 2 lbs.

- Lemon juice 2 tablespoons

- Parmesan cheese ½ cup

- Butter 4 tablespoons

- Mayonnaise 3 tablespoons

- Green onions 3 tablespoons

- Seasoning salt ¼ teaspoon

- Dried basil ¼ teaspoon

- Black and hot pepper

Directions

1. Preheat the oven to 350 degrees Fahrenheit.

2. Arrange the fillets in a single layer in a buttered 13-by-9-inch baking dish, or jellyroll tray.

3. Fillets should not be stacked.

4. Apply some juice to the tip.

5. Combine the cheese, sugar, mayonnaise, onions, and seasonings in a mixing bowl.

6. Using a fork, carefully mix the products.

7. Bake the fish for 10 to 20 minutes in a preheated oven, or until it begins to flake.

8. Spread the cheese mixture on top and bake for 5 minutes, or until golden brown.

9. The amount of time it takes to roast the fish can be calculated by its thickness.

10. Keep an eye on the fish to make sure it doesn't overcook.

12.4 Cauliflower Popcorn

Servings: 4 | Ready in 1 hr. 10 mins

Ingredients

- Cauliflower 1 head

- Olive oil 4 tablespoons

- Salt 1 teaspoon

Directions

1. Preheat the oven to 425 degrees Fahrenheit.

2. Trim the cauliflower head, discarding the thick and core stems; split the florets into Ping-Pong ball-sized bits.

3. Stir together the olive oil and salt in a wide mixing bowl, then add the cauliflower parts and toss well.

4. Spread the cauliflower parts on a baking sheet lined with parchment for quick cleaning, then roast for 1 hour, rotating 3 or 4 times until most of each portion has become golden brown.

5. Serve right away and enjoy.

12.5 Baked Potato

Servings: 1 | Ready in 1 hr. 10 mins

Ingredients

- Canola oil

- Salt

- Russet potato 1 large

Directions

1. Preheat the oven to 350 degrees Fahrenheit and put racks in the top and bottom thirds.

2. Wash the potatoes thoroughly under cool running water with a stiff brush.

3. Dry the spud, then poke 8 to 12 deep holes over it with a regular fork to permit moisture to escape while cooking.

4. Put in a bowl with a thin coating of oil.

5. Season with kosher salt and put directly on the oven's middle shelf.

6. To capture some drippings, place a baking sheet on the lower shelf.

7. Bake for 1 hour, or until the skin is crisp, but the flesh underneath is soft.

8. Serve by drawing a dotted line with your fork from end to end, then squeezing the ends together to break the potato open.

9. It will easily open.

12.6 Black Bean Soup

Servings: 4 | Ready in 25 mins

Ingredients

- Olive oil 3 tablespoons

- Medium onion 1

- Ground cumin 1 tablespoon

- Garlic 2-3 cloves

- Black beans 2 cans

- Chicken or vegetable broth 2 cups

- Red onion 1 small

- Salt and pepper

- Cilantro ¼ cup

Directions

1. In a pan, sauté the onion in olive oil.

2. Cumin can be applied until the onion turns transparent.

3. Cook for 30 seconds before adding the garlic and continuing to cook for another 30 to 60 seconds.

4. Add the 2 cups vegetable broth and 1 can of black beans.

5. Bring to low heat and cook, stirring periodically.

6. Turn the heat off.

7. Mix the ingredients in the pot with a hand blender or move to a blender.

8. Bring the second can of beans and the blended ingredients to a boil in the oven.

9. For garnish, serve the soup with bowls of red onion and cilantro.

12.7 Sauerkraut Salad

Servings: 6 | Ready in 15 mins

Ingredients

- Sauerkraut 1 lb.

- Celery 1 cup

- Green pepper ½ cup

- Onions 2 tablespoons, chopped

- Salt and pepper ½ teaspoon

- Sugar ¾ cup

- Salad oil 1/3 cup

- Cider 1/3 cup

Directions

1. Combine and mix the vegetables with the sauerkraut.

2. Heat oil, sugar, salt, vinegar, and pepper until the sugar melts.

3. Cool down and pour them over vegetables.

4. Leave to cool down overnight.

12.8 Hard-Boiled Eggs

Servings: 6 | Ready in 21 mins

Ingredients

- Water

- Large eggs 6

Directions

1. Place the eggs in a medium saucepan and fill with water. Place on high heat on the stovetop.

2. Get the water to a simmer. Remove it from heat and cover immediately. Allow for 18-20 minutes of resting time.

3. Keeping the pot on a slant, pour cold tap water into the pot, enabling the hot water to escape. Allow the eggs to stay in cold water for 1-2 mins before peeling.

12.9 Trail Mix

Servings: 6 | Ready in 2 mins

Ingredients

- Almonds 1 cup

- Sunflower seeds 1 cup

- Raisins 1 cup

- Dried apricot ½ cup

- Flaked coconut ¼ cup

- Chocolate ¼ cup

Directions

1. Combine all ingredients in an enormous container, cover, and shake.

2. Keep the container airtight. Refrigerate or freeze to preserve the necessary fatty acid properties.

12.10 Baked Mahi Mahi

Servings: 4 | Ready in 40 mins

Ingredients

- Mahi-mahi 2 lbs.

- Garlic salt ¼ teaspoon

- Lemon 1

- Ground pepper ¼ teaspoon

- Mayonnaise 1 cup

- White onion ¼ cup

- Breadcrumbs

Directions

1. Preheat the oven to 425 degrees Fahrenheit.

2. Place the fish in a baking dish after rinsing it. Squeeze lemon juice over the fish, then season with salt and pepper.

3. Spread mayonnaise and sliced onions on the fish. Bake for 25 minutes at 425°F with breadcrumbs on top.

12.11 Peach Berry Smoothie

Servings: 1 | Ready in 5 mins

Ingredients

- Frozen peaches 1 cup

- Coconut milk ¼ cup

- Greek yogurt ½ cup

- Almond flavoring ½ teaspoon

Directions

1. Mix peaches and almond flavoring in a blender.

2. Add milk to adjust the thickness.

3. Top with almond toppings and enjoy.

12.12 Millet & Quinoa Mediterranean Salad

Servings: 3-4 | Ready in 40 mins

Ingredients

- Millet ½ cup
- Water 1 cup
- Quinoa ½ cup
- Cucumber 1
- Tomatoes 1
- Sweet pepper 1
- Red onion ½
- Garlic 1 clove
- Feta cheese 200 g
- White beans 10 ounce
- Cayenne pepper ¼ teaspoon
- Dried dill 2 teaspoons
- Pine nuts ¼ cup
- Olive oil 1 tablespoon
- Lemon 1
- Ground pepper

Directions

1. Bring the millet and 1 cup of water to a boil, reduce to a low heat, and continue cooking for five minutes. Remove from heat, cover, and set aside for ten minutes.

2. Bring quinoa and 3/4 cup water to a boil, then reduce to low heat and cover and cook for 12-14 minutes, fluffing occasionally.

3. Mix both ingredients together and enjoy.

12.13 Poached Eggs and Avocado Toasts

Servings: 4 | Ready in 15 mins

Ingredients

- Eggs 4

- Avocados 2

- Lemon juice 2 teaspoons

- Thick bread 4 slices

- Cheese 1 cup

- Butter 4 teaspoons

- Salt and pepper

Directions

1. Use whatever tool you need to poach eggs.

2. Meanwhile, remove the stones from the avocados and break them in half.

3. Scoop out the flesh with a spoon and combine with the lemon or lime juice, salt, and pepper in a mixing bowl.

4. Using a fork, mash them together.

5. Bread should be toasted, and butter should be added to it.

6. Cover each slice of buttered toast with a dollop of avocado mixture and a poached egg.

7. Serve directly with a sprinkle of grated cheese on top.

8. On the side, serve with tomato halves, either new or fried.

12.14 Sheet Pan Chicken

Servings: 4 | Ready in 40 mins

Ingredients

- Chicken thighs 4

- Brussel sprouts 1 ½ cup

- Carrots 4

- Olive oil 3 tablespoons

- Herbs de Provence 1 teaspoon

Directions

1. Preheat the oven to 400 degrees Fahrenheit.

2. Place cut vegetables with 1 tablespoon of olive oil, 1 teaspoon of herbs, salt, and pepper in a dish. Rub the vegetables all over.

3. Arrange the vegetables on a sheet pan.

4. In the same dish, place the chicken thighs. Drizzle with 2 tablespoons of olive oil, 2 tablespoons of spices, and season with salt and pepper. Rub the chicken all over.

5. Place the chicken in the pan.

6. Roast for 30-35 minutes, or until the chicken is cooked through.

12.15 Berry Crisp

Servings: 6 | Ready in 45 mins

Ingredients

- Blueberries 16 ounces

- Sugar-free vanilla 7/8 ounce

- Cinnamon 1 teaspoon

- Nutmeg ½ teaspoon

- Non-fat milk ¼ cup

Crisp

- Oats 1 ½ cup

- Sugar ½ cup

- Fat-free yogurt 8 ounces

- Almond extract 1 teaspoon

Directions

1. Spray an 8x8 cooking pan.

2. In a pan, combine the fruit ingredients and stir well.

3. The crisp blend can be combined in a separate bowl.

4. To create a top crust, scatter this mixture over the berry mixture.

5. Preheat oven to 350°F and bake for 40-45 minutes, or until the topping is crunchy.

Conclusion

Intermittent fasting has been found to increase metabolism and fat burning while maintaining lean body mass, which will help with weight loss. When used in conjunction with other diets, such as the keto diet, it can help speed up ketosis and reduce harmful side effects like the keto flu. Intermittent fasting may be a healthy and reliable weight loss procedure, but it does not work for everyone.

Intermittent fasting may help people lose weight by decreasing total calorie intake, especially at night. It's possible, according to some scientists, that it would increase metabolism and fat burning. More study is required to learn more about the effects of intermittent fasting on our wellbeing and how it can be used to lose weight. There are also misconceptions regarding extended fasting and meal frequency. Many of these rumors, though, are false.

Smaller, more regular meals, for example, do not help you lose weight or improve your metabolism. Intermittent fasting is therefore far from dangerous, although it can have a range of advantages.

Women cannot benefit as much from intermittent fasting as men do. Women can adopt a relaxed approach to fasting, with shorter fasts and fewer fasting days, to minimize the harmful consequences. Intermittent fasting is a dietary practice that entails short-term fasts daily.

Regular 14–16-hour fasts, the 5:2 diet, or adapted alternate-day fasting are the safest for women. Although intermittent fasting has been seen to favor heart health, diabetes, and weight loss in some women, some research suggests it can have harmful effects on fertility and blood sugar levels in others.

Intermittent fasting is something to think about whether you're a woman trying to reduce weight or boost your wellbeing. Hormones play a part in nearly every element of your wellbeing. For the body to work correctly, you need them in exact quantities. Hormonal imbalances may also exacerbate obesity, diabetes, cardiac failure, and other health issues. Despite the reality that age and other causes are beyond your influence, you should take several measures to improve the hormones to work at their best. Consuming balanced meals, exercising often, and participating in other good habits will also help improve hormonal wellbeing.

Exercising when fasting is not only appropriate, but it is also beneficial for hormone optimization (which is essential for a variety of health benefits, including enhanced body composition). Mixing burst conditioning with intermittent fasting with a multi-therapeutic strategy will optimize the advantages of both. You can do cardio and weightlifting when fasted, but your results will suffer marginally in the short term.

Detox diets are said to help people shed weight by eliminating contaminants from their bodies. These diets, while appealing, are unnecessary because the body has its own highly effective detoxification mechanism. Staying hydrated, drinking less salt, staying healthy, and maintaining an antioxidant-rich diet will all support the body's natural detoxification mechanism and enhance your overall health.

To balance the body's normal circadian cycle, the safest time to work out when fasting is early in the day. Unless you're doing a lot of strenuous lifting or intense cardio, fasting during the workout will also help the hormones (for two to three hours). Fasting may be performed for several purposes, including faith, nutrition, or other health benefits. It is possible to exercise comfortably during IF.

Though IF and exercise can aid in weight reduction; there is mixed data on whether they are more successful than other methods, such as calorie restriction. Improved autophagy and potential anti-aging results are two possible advantages to fasting and exercise.

Printed in Great Britain
by Amazon